# Cybersecurity Fo

## Discover the Trade's Secret Attack Strategies And Learn Essential Prevention And Damage Control Mechanisms

## Yuri A. Bogachev

# Table Of Contents

# Introduction

The Information Superhighway gave way to what we know today as the Internet and opened the doors to the world of communication. This world resulted in digital networks worldwide connecting thoughts, ideas, cultures, web browsers, and websites.

The phrase "we are one" has become even more meaningful as the concept of the Internet is the core of how we communicate, conduct business, share art, music, videos, happenings in our lives, make things go viral and connect with the world.

The doors of the Internet opened another facet of communication that has necessitated the development and creation of cybersecurity. Our names, personally identifying information, bank accounts, credit cards and, in some cases, even our photos have all become targets for those using the Internet for their own nefarious purposes.

It was almost as soon as we were able to post our information, that they were working to be able to steal it. This gave birth to a new phrase–Internet fraud.

Internet fraud, scams, hacking, identity theft and the like have been the bane of almost anyone who has used the Internet. There are a fortunate few who have never been the victim of some type of information theft or getting locked out of computer or email browser, but they are only a few.

The majority of the billions of Internet users today have had some type of cyber fraud or virus perpetrated upon them, necessitating them to implement safeguards for their computers, tablets, and their cell phones to ward off what has become more than just an inconvenience.

The idea that you can go to what you may consider a "safe" website can be immediately shattered if your credit card or bank information is compromised.

Individuals are not the only victims of Internet fraud. Major corporations and businesses have been subject to data theft. Retailers, major credit bureaus, banks, and other institutions have had their fair share of hacking and viruses plague them. So, even if you personally protect your information, it still may be compromised if it is contained on another website.

Internet hackers, attackers, or crackers as they're known are usually interested in financial theft, yet there are those who hack into websites and steal information just for the fun of it. They may or may not do anything with the data they've stolen, but they revel in the idea that they can hack. For some of them, that feeling is enough and gives them the right to brag among their fellow hackers.

Today, we are dependent on the Internet for almost everything we do. It houses our contact information, our social media sites, credit card, and bank information—even the mediums we choose to get our news. Frankly, we're pretty much lost without our Internet lifeline and since that loss can be enormous, it's only right to protect it.

This book will be your guide and inform you of all the types of hazards that cybercriminals present to us as individuals and our own devices and to us through their attacks on major institutions that may hold our most personal and sensitive information in their systems.

Even television has jumped onto the insidiousness of the cybersecurity issues of today as a compelling storyline that gives us a warning. On *Grey's Anatomy*, Season 14, Episode 9, the hospital's entire computer system was shut down by a ransomware attack.

The episode showed how all cardio monitors, supply rooms secured by code, computers with all the data of the hospital, hospital staff and patients were held captive by a cybercriminal, whose message demanded to be paid by 5,000 bitcoins.

Hospital management misunderstood the payment to the attacker to be $5,000 and was immediately corrected by the FBI who let them know the ransom of 5,000 translated to a $20 million U.S.

Unfortunately, as you'll read later in the book, "*WannaCry*", an actual ransomware attack on May 12, 2017, disrupted the National Health Service (NHS), a Government-funded medical and health care service that citizens of the United Kingdom use as their health care facility.

The attack of the WannaCry expanded to more than 150 countries and the largest cyber-attack to hit NHS. However, the ransom demanded was in British pounds equivalent to $300 U.S. There is no evidence the ransom was paid, but the total cost of the attack remains unknown. (Cellan-Jones, Rory, 2017)

Learn how to protect your private and sensitive information, the types of attacks that cybercriminals perpetrate daily, and what the future of cybersecurity will mean to everyone who engages on the Internet.

# How To Get The Most Out Of This Book

This book has been written to work for you in a number of ways:

- Read the book in its entirety to gain all the information you need to have a full understanding of cybersecurity, the types of viruses, malware and other malicious software that can infect your personal devices, as well as the systems and networks of organizations worldwide.

- Use this book to follow the points of protection offered, and implement them to protect your devices from being attacked.

- Consider taking inventory of each of your devices and decide what plug-ins are absolutely needed, and which ones you should remove. If there are particular games you enjoy, that's fine. However, different versions of the same game leave your device and your personal data at risk.

- Help your family and friends understand how important it is to do all they can in protecting their personal data and the steps they need to take in order to do so. Become their expert in cybersecurity and recommend they read this book.

- The key is having a full and well-rounded understanding of cybersecurity and what it means to safeguard your personal information that's online. That is what this book wants to convey.

This book has been written for you to have full knowledge of the world of cybersecurity and how it affects you, your family, friends, and your industry. You need to be secure in the knowledge that everything is being done in this industry to protect your data and the data of all Internet users.

# Chapter 1: Welcome To The World Of Digital Security

## Cyberspace Concept

Cyberspace refers to the interconnected computer world and even more specifically, is an electronic means used to create a global computer network facilitating online communication. It is an interactive space encompassing networks that collect and store information digitally to make possible different forms of communication.

Cyberspace is a platform that is multifaceted. It is both an international and an individual concept and is a virtual and interactive setting for an extensive assortment of participants.

Individuals can network, relate, exchange ideas and information, offer social support, create artistic media, play games, do business, and participate in political ideologies while using a network that is worldwide.

The various facets of cyberspace are data and information, foundations, building blocks, and people.

## Data and Information

People look for data and information in cyberspace. Social media to interact with others, financial transactions, texts, news, videos—these are all types of information sought out by Internet users.

The data is deposited in various forms of media and is ready to be retrieved when a user desires it. The data is still stored in databases after it is used and can be adapted or controlled to comply with the creator or user's needs.

## Foundations

The cyberspace foundations include land cables, satellites, submarine cables and anything that offers a means of communication. Communication is possible through these transmission units.

Routers are also considered a foundation that makes sure the person requesting the information can access it while blocking out others' ability to view the requested data.

*Operating Systems*

The operating systems, web browsers and applications give us the ability to network with the foundations and access the data and information that we look for online.

These facets are what makeup cyberspace. All of them work together to permit us access to the Internet and to enable our wishes to meet our intents.

Don't confuse cyberspace with the web or the Internet. Although cyberspace is confused with the Internet, the term is really about the identities and objects that are within the communication network.

This means that all the happenings that are taking place on the Internet are real happenings in cyberspace, not in the locations where servers are physically located.

## Cybersecurity

*Cybersecurity—Its Origins*

The beginnings of cybersecurity were implemented for threats to computer security in the 1970s and 1980s. The threats of the time were not malicious but more in line with securing access from documents being read by those who shouldn't. The origins of cybersecurity emanated with a research project implemented by Bob Thomas.

Thomas recognized the ability of a computer program to leave a small trail wherever it went across a network. Naming the program "*Creeper*", Thomas designed it to cross between Tenex terminals on the ARPANET, the early version of the Internet, printing a message at all the terminals it visited.

Ray Tomlinson (the inventor of email) dabbled with the program and created a self-replicating one–the original computer worm. Once he achieved that end of the program, he created a separate program called "*Reaper*".

*Reaper* was the first antivirus software. It chased *Creeper* and deleted it. Thus, the beginning of cybersecurity.

In 1986 the Internet gateway was hacked in Berkeley and piggybacked on the ARPANET. This enabled a hacker by the name of Hess to hack 400 military computers, up to and including mainframes at the Pentagon. His intent was to sell United States secrets to the Russian KGB.

Fortunately, an astronomer by the name of Clifford Stoll identified the invasion and used a honeypot technique, a computer security system set to deflect or in some way counteract unauthorized attempts to information systems.

In 1988, Robert Morris decided he wanted to measure the size of the Internet. He wrote a program that was designed to transmit across networks, penetrate

Unix terminals with a known bug and then replicate itself. The last direction was a mistake. The Morris worm copied itself so forcefully that it slowed down an early Internet to a crawl and caused incalculable damage.

After the Morris worm, viruses began to become deadlier and affected more systems. By the late 1980s, the first trickle of security systems began appearing and by the early 1990s, there was a burst of security companies that offered AV scanners.

With the growth of Internet crime, scams, and viruses, cybersecurity became a full-blown industry.

Cybersecurity is defined as the protection methods used to guard computers and all the elements encompassed that can be attacked from illegal and unsanctioned access that are targeted for misuse and abuse.

The security of computer applications involves measures taken to safeguard applications that are menaced and filter through any defects in the plan of the application, distribution, development maintenance or upgrade. Some techniques used are:

- Authorization and Authentication
- Session management, exception management, and parameter administration
- Logging and auditing

Information security protects the data from being illegally accessed to prevent the theft of IDs and safeguarding privacy. The methods employed to implement security are:

- Identifying the user's permission and authentication
- Cryptography

Recovery planning for disasters includes the assessment of risk, setting priorities, and establishing strategies for recovery in the event of a disaster. Businesses, in particular, should have a solid plan for recovery in the event of a disaster to proceed with normal operations of the business as fast as possible after the disaster is remedied. (*Economic Times* staff, 2019)

Network security protects its dependability, honesty, usability, and security. It focuses on varied dangers and detains the threats from engaging or expanding through the network. The protection components of recovery planning are:

- Firewall—blocks unsanctioned, unauthorized access to your network

- Anti-spyware and anti-virus

- (VPNs) Virtual Private Networks to offer secure remote connection

- Intrusion Prevention Systems (IPS) to pinpoint threats that are a fast-spreading

*The Importance of Cybersecurity*

There isn't anyone who uses the Internet, whether as an individual or a business, who likes getting hacked. Everyone is affected by getting hacked, data is compromised, and if you're not able to retrieve your information, personal or otherwise, photos and the like are lost forever and information to your identity and financial institutions fall into the wrong hands.

Businesses that are hacked are not just inconvenienced, but their clients are at risk as well.

Companies are faced with the possibility of being in legal jeopardy because of cybercrime.

If a company suffers a full-scale assault and its customers' personal and financial information is comprised, the level of legal action taken against the company can end the company's solvency due to lawsuits.

The government is most concerned about malicious actors invading their information. The highest of confidential data can be stolen from anywhere in the world. In one database compromise, the personal information of approximately half of the U.S. was breached by the attack on Equifax, a credit reporting company. (Stokdyk, 2018)

With increasingly more gadgets created that use the Internet to operate, there is a danger of cybercrime becoming more serious. Self-driving cars and home security systems that are Internet-enabled all are in danger of being hacked.

*Some Cybersecurity Facts*

There is a hacker attack every 39 seconds on average according to a Clark School study at the University of Maryland. One in three Americans is affected by these attacks annually.

The most common reason for attacks? The non-secure usernames and passwords most people use. This is one of the main opportunities given to attackers for success. Using a non-decipherable username or password is a good way to lessen the possibility of being hacked.

Additionally, there are only three industries that 95% of breached information came from. Retail, technology, and government industries are popular targets not because they are less diligent in protecting their clients' data, but because the level of personal information that is contained in their systems is very high. (Milkovich, Devon, 2019)

## Types of Cyber Attacks

Over the course of the book, an explanation of some of the most common attacks will be addressed. Some of these attacks are:

- DoS–Denial-of-Service
- DDoS–Distributed Denial-of-Service
- Phishing and Spear Phishing
- MitM—Man-in-the-Middle
- Password attack
- SQL injection attack
- Eavesdropping attack
- Snooping attack

## Low Hanging Fruit of the Internet

Envision a fruit tree like oranges or apples with branches of the tree laden in fruit low enough that you can easily reach up and get an apple or an orange. This means the fruit is easily reached by someone who wants to grab some fruit.

The phrase is used to point out that the fruit is equal to rewards and the rewards are pretty easy to get in comparison to fruit that is higher up the tree. (Programmer Interview staff, 2019)

Internet service providers–Chrome, Firefox, and Internet Explorer are low hanging fruit on the Internet. Many people do not have their service provider configured for privacy.

In order to configure your privacy settings to protect your privacy, here are the ways to configure each server:

*Chrome*

- Open your computer to Chrome.
- At the top right of the browser click on More Settings.

- Click on Advanced at the bottom.

- Beneath "Privacy and Security" there are settings that you can choose to turn off. Click on Site settings to regulate the way Chrome handles permissions and content.

*Firefox*

- Access Firefox.

- Go to the upper righthand corner and click on Settings, the three horizontal lines, to get a drop-down menu.

- Under Options, click on the Security tab.

- Manage the Security Settings–You want to be alerted when sites install add-ons, block reported attach sites, block web forgeries.

- Passwords–It is up to you if you want the sites that you visit to remember your passwords or not.

- Master Password–A master password under Security allows you to decide if you want to create a master password to access your saved passwords and usernames on Firefox.

- When you've completed making your choices, click on the OK button. This will update your security on Firefox.

*Internet Explorer*

- Access Internet Explorer.

- Select the button marked Tools, then select the Security tab.

- To have your security zone settings customized, choose the zone icon. Move the slider to the security level you would like.

We all want our privacy maintained, especially when we are navigating on the Internet. Consider all the protective options that are available to protect all your devices from being hacked or infected with viruses.

# Chapter 2: Making Sense Of Encryption

## What is Encryption?

Encryption is a mystery to most Internet users. Unless you have an Information Security degree or have a keen interest in what encryption is, it remains one of the necessary enigmas of security.

The conversion of information into a cryptographic code that is unable to be read without a key is encryption. The encrypted data appears to be meaningless, is made to be challenging and is very hard to decipher without a key.

Encryption is a process. The process converts information or data into code, specifically to prevent unauthorized entry. It is used to protect transmitted information online. (Lexico Dictionary, 2019)

Some examples of encryption are:

*Communication*–Links that communicate between a website and a browser are encrypted and use Secure Sockets Layer (SSL). The messages that travel between a website and browser travel extensive distances and through a number of machines. The messages are encrypted to avert the possibility of anyone accessing the data that is being sent between the sender and receiver.

*Digital Certificates*—These certificates are a way of pinpointing and confirming the identity of information services. For example, a company publishes its name and a digital certificate with a public key is issued by a certificate authority.

*Devices*—Mobile phones are devices that may be constructed by default to use encrypted data storage.

*Filesystems*–A hard drive, which is a filesystem in a laptop, can be encrypted with a password in order to access data.

Encryption is converted into cryptographic encoding that cannot be read without the correct key.

## What is Cryptography?

Cryptography is the creation of codes that are generated or written to permit transmissions to travel through cyberspace incognito. It transforms data into an unreadable form for unapproved and unlawful users.

This lets the data be transmitted without any unauthorized person decoding it into a readable format that would comprise the data. (Techopedia, 2019)

*Example–Passwords.* We type them into different accounts. Typing a password with letters and numbers that then become encrypted gives access to the website that recognizes it. Banks, credit cards, our computers–anywhere we need to use a password for access.

Cryptography is used on several levels for information security. A decryption key is needed to read the information. Without the correct key, the information can't be read, traversing uncompromised and while being stored.

The sender and delivery can be verified by cryptography, which is used as an aid to nonrepudiation. Cryptology is also a name known for cryptography.

Cryptography has various kinds of algorithms for encryption. They are:

*Symmetric Encryption*–also known as SKC, Secret Key Cryptography. This allows for only one key to encrypt and decrypt information.

*Asymmetric Encryption*–this encryption type is also known as PKC, Public Key Cryptography. This encryption uses two keys: a public key allowing entry by anyone, and a private key where it can be accessed by the possessor of the key alone.

A sender has the information encrypted by the recipient's public key. The recipient decrypts the message using the private key.

For non-renunciation, the plain text is encrypted via a private key by the sender and decrypts it by the public key. This assures the recipient of knowing where the data came from. (Milkovich, Devon, 2019)

*Symmetric and Asymmetric Key Cryptography– What's the Difference?*

The basic difference that makes each of these encryptions distinct is their key. The symmetric encryption allows both the encryption and decryption of a message with the same key, while asymmetric key cryptography uses two keys.

The Symmetric Key Cryptography

- Uses single or same key for encryption and encryption

- This key is quicker than asymmetric key cryptography

- A sender encrypts plain text using a shared secret key

- A ciphertext is transmitted through the Internet

- The ciphertext is decrypted by the receiver using the same decryption key receive the original plain text

The Asymmetric Key Cryptography

- Uses two keys—one for encryption and the other for decryption

- One key is a public key that may be known to everyone. This key is used to encrypt messages and authenticate signatures. The other key is private and only known to the receiver of the message (or verifier) and used to decrypt messages. It can also create signatures.

- The key used for decryption must correspond with the encryption key. No other key can decrypt the message.

- Although the sender and receiver can use the encryption key (public) and have the ability to verify signatures or encrypt messages, the sender cannot create signatures or decrypt messages because the receiver is the only one who knows the decryption key (private).

## What is Data Encryption and What Is Its Role?

The translation of data into another form or code is encryption. Only the individuals with access to a decryption key or a password have the ability to read it.

Data that is encrypted is known as ciphertext while unencrypted data is known as plaintext. The data (plaintext) is encrypted. The encryption key and algorithm transform the plaintext into ciphertext. The ciphertext can only be seen in its original form when it is decrypted with the correct key. (Lord, Nate, 2019)

Organizations use encryption as the most effective way to secure data. Data encryption is probably the most important function that can be used to protect digital data confidentiality transmitted over the Internet or other computer networks, and stored in computer systems.

Data encryption that is outdated is now replaced by encryption algorithms that are more state-of-the-art. They play a crucial role in the security of communications and IT systems.

Confidentiality and drive key security actions to include integrity, authentication, and non-repudiation. The message's origin is verified by authentication while proof that a message's content has not been changed is provided by integrity. Finally, so that the sender cannot deny sending the message, it is ensured by non-repudiation. (Lord, Nate, 2019)

## Challenges of Encryption Protocols

One of the most basic ways to attack encryption is by brute force or attempting to try random keys until the correct key is located. The possible number of keys is determined by the length of the key and can affect the likelihood of this kind of attack.

Remember that encryption strength directly corresponds to key size. However, as the size of the key increases, so too do the number of resources that are needed to execute the computation.

Side-channel attacks and cryptanalysis are methods of breaking a cipher.

*Side-channel attack*–This attacks the application of the cipher, not the cipher itself. If there is an error in execution or system design, the attacks may be successful.

*Cryptanalysis*–This attack seeks a weakness in a cipher and capitalizes on it. When there is a flaw in the cipher, this type of attack can be applied. (Lord, Nate, 2019)

## Encryption Mistakes

Today, there are dynamic Internet security tools that aid us in remaining private, anonymous and detain disruptive and unauthorized entities from getting hold of our information and business.

Digital encryption is one of the support systems upon which the modern web is built. It is a fast and effective way to diminish the breaches of trust and fraud on the Internet.

However, like everything that happens in life, it is only good as the person responsible for wielding it. Encryption can be incorrectly used. Mistakes can be made in various ways that can compromise the security and benefits that are employed when using encryption technology.

Providers should know about these errors and users should hold providers accountable because providers should be aware of mistakes that are made from the beginning.

Some of the common encryption mistakes are:

*Using Encryption That's Obsolete*—Really smart people develop encryption algorithms, yet someone will figure out how to thrash them. It's not just the unauthorized bad entities who are trying to defeat these encryptions. Researchers who specialize in encryption security look for encryption that is vulnerable so any problems can be remedied before the weakness is discovered.

Internet routers are an example of how these weaknesses can happen. WPA2 is the current standard for encrypting the Wi-Fi signal between the router and your device.

Prior to this encryption, WEP and WPA were used. These two are considered less secure and obsolete. However, due to compatibility issues, they are included in modern routers, but the instances of WEP being cracked are negligible these days.

Another encryption that has become obsolete is the Data Encryption Standard or DES. This encryption has been cracked since the 1990s.

Today, we have the Advanced Encryption Standard or AES. There are no practical ways to crack AES even though there have been imaginative attacks that have been created in an attempt to crack it.

AES is what is considered the gold standard, although the KRACK attack is being considered a serious concern.

If encryption has a practical crack, don't use it.

*Not Using the Correct Expertise*—Coders are incredible problem solvers and are very smart. They are one of the invaluable resources of the digital world. However, they may not know how to set up encryption correctly with all the fail-safes, checks and balances that should be in place.

This is a critical error that many companies who suffer data breaches have made. They admit that the implementation of their data security was not performed by experts in encryption security and didn't have the expertise to know how to execute data security correctly.

Hire the services of security specialists who are validated to implement encryption solutions. They can confer with your developers to develop secure solutions. (Butler, 2018)

## Myths About Data Encryption

There are many preconceptions that still impede companies from incorporating encryption solutions to have their data protected. The irony of this mindset is that without securing data with encryption, it could be more costly if there *is* a huge data leak, including the possibility of a business losing clients and business because of the legal ramifications that can arise from a data breach.

These are some of the most common myths about data encryption:

*It's a Waste of Money to Encrypt Data*–Having data encryption is like car insurance. You only need it when you have an accident. However, a study conducted by Ponemno Institute for IBM, 2018: Cost of a Data Breach Study: Global View found that in France the cost of data theft is €3.54 million Euros ($3.93 million U.S.). This was an increase from 2017 to 8.2%.

Companies cannot afford to dismiss the potential sources of vulnerability. This includes document sharing services that are cloud-based and employee nomadism.

*It's Too Complicated to Set Up Encryption*–Until recently, data protection was a complex procedure that discouraged many.

However, today there are solutions offered by publishers that no longer need the implementation of an infrastructure that is too complex. New solutions have made the implementation and management of encryption systems clearer.

SaaS mode has made it possible for significantly lower maintenance and infrastructure costs.

*I May Never Get My Data Back If I Encrypt It*–The fear many people have is they might lose their data if they forget their password, or if someone leaves the company and forgets to give someone their password before they leave.

However, there are technologies that can aid in preventing this such as data recovery. This offers one or two people within company access in the event of imperative need.

Another possibility is the key escrow technique where an encrypted database is used to store a company's encryption keys.

Realize that it is much more costly to have a breach of data security than having data protection. The technology has become much simpler than years past. (Krystlik, 2019)

No one is totally safe from cyber-attacks and one of the most effective protection systems is encryption. This demonstrates that really nothing should impede companies from accepting sound encryption solutions.

# Chapter 3: Locked Out Of Your System–Dealing With The Dangers

There are some things that give us a sinking feeling in our stomach. You may have gone for a ride on a ridiculously high and twisty roller coaster, saw what lay ahead, and when you reached the top there was no way to go but down.

Or, you may have missed the last train for the evening and don't have enough money for an expensive cab ride. You misplaced your car keys and there isn't a spare key.

You lock yourself out of your house and you only have your pajamas on and no shoes; it's winter. You lose your wallet with all your ID, money, and other information that you should have kept at home in a safe place.

Or, you just turned on your computer and found that you were locked out of your system. You're not only locked out, but you haven't a clue as to how it happened, or how to be able to get back in. Here comes that sinking feeling.

## Locked Out of Your System

A global virtual environment, mostly on the Internet, created by computer systems is what cyberspace is.

The working principle of cyber-attacks is actions that are offensive and target infrastructures, computer information systems, personal computer devices or computer networks.

The attacks use several varied methods to alter, steal, or maliciously controlling a computing system to destroy the integrity of data and information systems or data.

There are 10 common kinds of cyber-attacks:

- Denial-of-Service, DoS and Distributed Denial-of-Service, DDoS attacks

- Phishing and Spear Phishing attacks

- Man-in-the-Middle, MitM attack

- Drive-by attack

- Cross-site scripting, XSS attack

- SQL injection attack

- Password attack

- Eavesdropping attack

- Malware attack

- Birthday attack

*A DoS Attack*

This attack is a cyber-attack that disables a computer or system and makes them inaccessible. The disruption of the services of a source that has a link to the Internet can be temporary or indefinite. (Wikipedia, 2019)

The attack occurs when a great number of computers open a website, flooding the website with too much traffic flowing to it and denying access to everyone else trying to access the website.

Many web companies were attacked by DoS in the 1990s and early 2000s. An example of this is when Microsoft had a DoS attack affect them in 2001. Users were unable to access Microsoft's website and many other services provided by Microsoft.

In 2014, a DDoS attack was targeted at Evernote which lasted 24 hours.

This attack doesn't really offer direct benefits to the attacker. The satisfaction for them is that they have created a service denial. If, however, the resource that's attacked is a business competitor to the attacker, then the attacker reaps the benefit of compromising confidential company data. (Melnick, Jeff, 2018)

There are different types of DoS attacks:

*TCP SYN flood attack*—An attack where the attacker exploits using the buffer space during the TCP (Transmission Control Protocol) handshake initialization.

A system that has too many people trying to connect all at once flood the targeted system and it gets too much Internet traffic. The Internet servers get slowed, cannot respond when it tries to reply to requests and then ultimately it stops and crashes.

As an antidote to an attack:

- A firewall that can be configured to halt the attack can be placed in front of the servers.

- Decrease timeout on open connections and have the size of the connection queue increased.

*Teardrop attack*—There are bugs in software or systems in Internet packets that are sent to attack. These are fragmented packets to target a machine. If the total of the size and offset of a fragmented packet is different from that of the next packet, the packets overlap. (Melnick, Jeff, 2018)

Firewalls or software patches usually are able to correct the problem and this type of attack is easier to defend.

*Smurf attack*—also known DDoS attack where there is a deluge of messages that are spoofed. These messages target the IP address of the victim.

A victim's network hosts answer the ICMP (Internet Control Message Protocol) request. Increased traffic develops on the target network making it crash.

Preventing an attack:

Configure separate routers as well as hosts to remain non-responsive toward broadcasts or external ping requests. Configure routers to make sure packets are not forwarded to the directed broadcast addresses. This will prevent a Smurf attack.

*Ping of Death attack*–This attack pings an IP size that is beyond 65,635 bytes. The attacker fragments the IP packets because the size of these packets isn't permissible. A target system can experience buffer overflow and crashes when the system reassembles the packet.

To block a Ping of Death attack:

The way to block a Ping of Death attack is to use a firewall that will check the maximum size of fragmented IP packets.

*Botnets*—These are used by hackers to carry out DDoS attacks. The botnets are malware that infects millions of systems. They are known as bots or zombie systems. Target systems are attacked by bots and have their processing capabilities and bandwidth overwhelmed.

To Mitigate Botnets:

Deny traffic from spoofed addresses with RFC3704 filtering. The correct source network will be ensured of receiving traceable traffic.

The BGP (Border Gateway Protocol) host sends traffic through the ISP routers, who protect victim servers by routing all traffic updates and can identify a DDoS attack. It drops unwanted traffic before it gets into a protected network and filters it into a black hole.

Getting locked out of your system is beyond inconvenient and dangerous. If it's your company computer, the problem may be systemwide and a problem that may need to be remedied in the mainframe. If it's your own PC, laptop or tablet, the danger of your personal information being compromised is very real.

There are several ways to lock your computer to prevent others from seeing what information you have in the system or on the last screen you had up. The same applies to your phones. Lock them up when you are not using it. (Melnick, Jeff, 2018)

## Locking Your Computer

Leaving your computer and/or phone unlocked can leave you open to anyone having access to information that is private, or if you're at work and work on confidential files, anyone interested in what's confidential may be able to access those files.

Whether it's five minutes to go to the restroom or its lunchtime and you'll be back in 45 minutes, locking your computer keeps your data secure and any prying eyes away

*To Lock Your PC or Laptop:*

- Click on CTRL + ALT + DELETE keys simultaneously. Hold all three for a few seconds and then choose "Lock" or "Lock Computer" from the menu.

- Another way to lock your computer is by pressing the "Windows" key and "L" simultaneously.

*To Lock Your MAC:*

If your MAC is running macOS High Sierra, go to the Apple menu. Press "Command" + "Control" + Q.

Another way to lock your MAC running macOS High Sierra is to go to the Apple menu and choose Lock Screen.

Older versions of the MAC operating system press "Control" + "Shift" + "Power" keys.

**Lock Your Phone**

*Locking your iPhone*

- To lock an iPhone 6 and later models press the Sleep/Wake button. You can find this on the right side of the device.

Changing iPhone Lock Settings:

- Go to Settings and tap Touch ID and Passcode found on the menu. The screen permits you to set a passcode.

- You are able to choose between a 4-digit code that contains only numbers, letters and numbers or a custom code of numbers.

- Newer iPhones also have the ability to use Touch ID or a fingerprint to unlock the phone.

*Locking your Android*

- Press the power button. This is the usual way to lock the Android phone screen.

Changing Android Lock Settings:

- Tap the Menu button on the Home Screen, then choose Settings.

- Choose Security or Location & Security for Android 5.0 and earlier models.

- Scroll down to the Screen Lock option. The words may vary from one phone to another depending on the manufacturer.

- A choice between PIN, password or pattern may be the choice.

Always lock your devices that have personal and sensitive data. Computers, mobile phones, and tablets all need to be locked.

Automatically locking your device is what most devices have after a period of inactivity. If you forget to lock your computer, this is a great feature

Some apps on your phone may be able to be restricted or locked with settings that are built into your phone (RTI Staff, 2019)

## Locked Out of His Email Account

A friend of mine, Mark, is a professional musician. He signed on to his email account one morning and could not get in. He began to get frustrated because he depends on emails to get offers for work. He is also a private music teacher. The Internet and his emails were the way he communicated with his many students around the world.

While Mark was in the midst of trying to figure out how to get into his email account, the doorbell rings. He answers the door and greeted another musician, Catherine, with whom he had recently performed in her musical revue the month before.

Catherine was startled and proclaimed, "Oh, you're here! I was worried. I just received an email saying you were stuck in Africa, had your money stolen and could I help out by sending $200 to you. If I could, you would give me directions as to how I could send it to you."

It all began to make sense to Mark. Someone had hacked into his email and was emailing all his contacts with the same stuck in Africa story and asking them to send money.

Fortunately for Mark, he had another email account with the same contacts. He sent out a group email to all his contacts to forewarn them of this scam email and not to respond to it.

Mark asked Catherine to forward the scam email to his useable email account and responded to the scammer. He let the scammer know he was on to him and he wouldn't be receiving any money.

Mark then tried to recover his emails from his locked account but had no luck. He followed the directions his email server, typed in the most recent password he remembered and knew what it was, and also got asked when he set up the account. He couldn't remember the month or year and with that, Mark's email account was compromised and gone.

Getting locked out of your email or your system is the worst, and unfortunately, it happens to practically everyone at one point or another.

# Chapter 4: Unmasking The Man-In-The-Middle

What happens when an adversary plants themselves in the middle of two parties, let's say a title company that receives funds for the purchase of homes, and the party who is purchasing the home?

The home buyer is instructed to have the funds for the payment of the home be transmitted from their bank to the title company's bank account. However, the adversary has placed themselves between the buyer and the title company and they receive the money instead. The email account of the title company has been hacked.

The title company's email account is monitored by the hacker for the names of the parties involved with the property being purchased—the names of the real estate agents, the names of the buyers and sellers, the title company's name, the scheduled time and date of the closing, and when the funds are needed to be received by the title company.

The hacker contacts the buyers via email a few days before the deadline of the wire transfer to the title company's bank account and gives the buyers instructions to wire the money to a different bank account. The email is disguised as the title company's legitimate emails that have been previously sent to the buyers so there is no suspicion on the part of the buyers that the email is fraudulent.

The buyers have no way of knowing that their funds were never received into the title company's bank account because they receive the fraudulent email stating their funds were received.

It is only when the title company contacts the buyers to say the title company's bank account has no record of receiving the funds and the purchase cannot be closed until the funds are received. It's at this moment they realize they've been a victim of a real estate closing scam and the title company is the victim of a hacker.

## How Does MitM Attack Actually Work?

This is one of the oldest forms of cyber-attacks. The attack, also known as MitM, is when an adversary manipulates a transmission between two parties. The two parties believe they are contacting one another directly, while the Man-in-the-Middle is the one who is communicating one or both of the parties. (Swinhoe, Dan, 2019)

MitM attacks are hard to detect, but there are ways that they can be prevented.

Ways to prevent these threat actors from eavesdropping or tampering with communications have been sought by computer scientists since the early 1980s. MitM attacks are where the attacker is virtually sitting between a legitimate host and the victim who is trying to connect to the host. The attacker is either intercepting the connection, ending that connection and creating a new connection to the host or they're passively listening in by either eavesdropping secretly or modifying the traffic that travels between them.

The communication is either traffic that is manipulated or observed. This could be by creating fake networks that the attacker controls, or through the interference with legitimate networks.

This type of attack is used to steal personal information, credentials to log in a confidential site, spy on a party or have the communications data sabotaged or corrupted.

Although there is protection against MitM attacks with encryption, attackers who are successful will pass on the traffic to the destination it was intended to be received after it's been recorded or harvested, thus not leaving any means of detection of an attack.

However, the attacker can also take the traffic and reroute it to phishing sites. These sites are designed to appear legitimate and have the receiver engage with it as they would with the website the phishing site represents.

Traffic becomes compromised and stripped of any encryption so the attacker can steal, reroute or change the traffic to the destination that an attacker chooses. A destination can be a phishing log-in site.

Silently observed or re-encrypted intercepted traffic to the intended source can be recorded or edited by the attackers making it hard to spot the attack.

There is a vast range of techniques and possible outcomes encompassed by MitM. An example of this is an HTTPS connection established between the attacker and the server in SSL stripping, but with an HTTP connection that is unsecured with the user, information is sent in plain text without encryption.

Legitimate Wi-Fi access points are mirrored by Evil Twin attacks but are controlled totally by malicious actors who can collect, monitor or manipulate all the information the user sends.

If a user is making a bank transfer, an attacker can see that transfer is made, change the amount being sent or the account number of the destination. MitM attacks can gather login credentials or personal information.

Attackers who notice that applications are being downloaded or updated, updates that are compromised that install malware can be sent in place of the legitimate ones.

The exploit kit *EvilGrade* was explicitly designed to target updates that are poorly secured. They frequently fail to have traffic encrypted. Mobile devices are especially susceptible to this type of attack.

*MitM Types of Attacks*

There are two forms of MitM attacks–the first is physical adjacency to an intended target and the other is malicious malware or software.

The second form, like the fake bank transfer example, is called a Man-in-the-Browser attack. Cybercriminals usually implement an attack in two phases–interception and decryption.

There are several ways that cybercriminals use MitM attacks to gain control of devices.

*Session Hijacking*–This is a security attack on a protected network during a user session. The most common session hijacking method is IP spoofing. (Geeks for Geeks, 2019)

*IP Spoofing*–An identifying Internet Protocol (IP) address, which is similar to your home address, is found in every device that has the ability to connect to the Internet.

When an IP address is spoofed, an attacker tricks you into thinking you're communicating with a website or another individual but you're not—and possibly allowing access to the information you wouldn't share otherwise. (Symantec employee, 2019)

*Replay Attack*–This is when an attacker detects the transmission of data and has it fraudulently repeated or delayed. The repeat or delay of transmitted data by a malicious entity or the sender seizes the transmission and resends the fraudulent transmission. (Techopedia, 2019)

Replay attacks fool parties into believing they've successfully completed the data transmission while the attack on the security protocol using replays of data transmission that's from a different sender is transmitted into the receiving system of the intended recipient.

A replay attack is also known as a Playback attack.

Networks and computers that have been subject to a replay attack would see the attack appear as legitimate messages. A replay attack gains entry to the resources by an authentication message being replayed and confusing the destination host.

## How to Execute a MitM Attack in 15 Minutes

A Man-in-the-Middle attack happens when a third-party adversary places itself in the center of a connection. It's presented usually in the context of a Wi-Fi network that's public. (The SSL store, 2019)

In order to execute a MitM attack, an understanding of the Internet needs to be clarified.

There is a misunderstanding about the Internet and the nature of connections. When the average Internet user is asked how they connect to a website and are asked to draw a map, it's usually going to be from their computer to the website in one straight line. Some may include a router or a modem or their ISP to the map but after those may be added, the map proceeds straight to the website.

However, the map is actually more complicated to reach a single website. When a URL is typed into the address bar, the browser sends a request called a Domain Name Server (DNS).

The browser shows the IP address that's associated with the URL that is trying to be reached and finds the fastest way there.

Actually, to reach a website it takes more than going from point A to point B.

When Internet users think about hackers, they think of the usual photos of hackers wearing a hoodie pulled over their heads in a dark room. Factually, hackers are in their office or apartment with lights and windows reflecting light. They may wear hoodies, but they don't have them pulled up on their heads.

Hacking is not that difficult, it's more common than people think and the barrier to access is very low.

Most of the information that is needed to create a MitM attack can be found on Google.

SHODAN is the Sentient Hyper-Optimized Data Access Network. Almost any device that is connected to the Internet can be located by this search engine. In this context, a banner is a snippet of information that relates to the device itself.

SHODAN port returns information on any device that hasn't been specially secured after the port scans the Internet.

The items not secured are IP addresses, device names, firmware versions, manufacturers and the like.

When you stop to consider all the ways SHODAN can be misused, it can be pretty scary—terrifying, actually. A search can be narrowed down to particular locations, going as granular as coordinates for a GPS with the right commands.

Specific devices can be located if you have their IP addresses.

With SHODAN there is a means to be able to track down specific devices and look for MitM high volume targets. Quite a few still use their default settings and are unsecured.

Those default settings are pretty easily found, especially the Admin ID and password with the use of Google.

If the device's make and model can be figured out from the banner, finding the default of the information is not a problem.

Once you decide on the device, a search on Google for the default password/ID will give the necessary information. Unauthorized access can now be gained to any unsecured device and perform the MitM attack.

*Type in Google search: (the device you wish to find the password for) default password. *Example*: Type in search Samsung default password. This will give you the Samsung default passwords and default IP address

The next step is the packet sniffers. Data is not being sent in a steady stream across the Internet.

The data doesn't flow forward in a straight, steady stream. Information is being broken down and encoded into packets of data and transmitted. The inspection of these packets of data is performed by a Packet Sniffer. It can tell if the data is not encrypted.

*Google Packet Sniffers*—A quick search on GitHub brings up several results of Packet Sniffers readily available on the Internet.

Every device is not going to work nicely with Packet Sniffers, but with a search on Google eventually finding the right fit won't be that hard.

There are options that can be used. Locate a Packet Sniffer that will coordinate directly into the device we're hacking requires very little configuration by us. Or, new firmware can be placed on the device and we can build out some added functionality if we want to go for broke.

This will bring all these actions full circle. After the attacker has located an unsecured device, found the default login information that's needed to access the device by pulling its banner, the next step is to install a Packet Sniffer or any malware they choose. Any information passing through that gateway can eavesdrop on any information. Or worse. (The SSL store, 2019)

MitM attacks are executed for financial gain, spying, or just to be disruptive. They can cause small or enormous damage all depending on what the goals of the attacker are and their ability and desire to cause chaos.

# Chapter 5: How Your Personal Data Is Stolen By Exploiting Your Trust

The commonplace occurrence of data breaches now has desensitized people to the news that another data breach has occurred, causing companies to scramble to shore up the damage and do everything to regain the trust of consumers and clients whose data was compromised by the breach.

It is no longer required by companies just to make an announcement that their systems have been breached, but to pay fines that can be up to 4% of their annual turnover should the data belonging to citizens of the EU (European Union) made by the requirements of the GDPR (General Data Protection Regulation).

Lawsuits abound with some companies because the data is so sensitive that some clients stand to lose millions because of a data breach.

## Data Breach—What It Is and How It Affects You

When a cybercriminal is successful in infiltrating a data source and takes sensitive information, this is how a data breach happens. Accessing a computer or network to steal local files can be done physically or by having the ability to remotely bypass network security. (Trend Micro, 2018)

Remotely bypassing network security is the usual method used when targeting companies.

These are the steps taken in a typical breach action:

*The Research*—Weaknesses in a company's security—either systems, people, or the network are scoped out by the cybercriminal.

*The Attack*—Initial contact is made either using a network or social attack by the cybercriminal.

*Network or Social Attacks*—When a cybercriminal infiltrates an infrastructure system and application weaknesses to attack an organization's network, a network attack happens.

Baiting or tricking employees into relinquishing access to the company's network is a social attack. An employee can be fooled and open a malicious attachment or tricked into giving their login credentials.

*Exfiltration*—The cybercriminal can attack the network and work their way to confidential company data and compromise it by getting into only one computer. When the data is extracted the attack is considered successful by the hacker.

**Types of Data Breach Attacks**

*Phishing attack*—This type of attack is when a cybercriminal sends emails that have the appearance of being from a trusted source. For example, sending an email with a bank logo to the bank's customer. (Melnick, Jeff, 2018)

The goal of sending an email is to influence users to do something or to gain personal information from users. This type of attack is a combination of technical trickery and social engineering.

The attack may involve an email that has an attachment that loads malware onto a user's computer. Or, it can be a trick to click a link to a deceiving website, tricking the user to give out their personal information or download malware onto their computer.

*Spear Phishing*—This attack is a phishing activity that is very targeted. Research is conducted and targets and messages that are relevant and personal are created by attackers. This type of attack is difficult to identify and even more difficult to have a defense against.

A simple way to execute spear phishing can be implemented when email spoofing is performed. The "From" line is false information and appears to be from someone you know, such as your partner company or management.

Another method that scammers use is copying real websites that are duplicated to dupe you into typing in your login credentials or personally identifiable information. (Melnick, Jeff, 2018)

## How Our Personal Data Gets Compromised

There are many ways in which data that is extremely personal to us can be compromised. There are reasons that data compromise can occur and some of them are out of our control.

*Organization Data Breach*—Organizations frequently need our personal information in order to do business with us. Financial institutions, retail stores, medical groups, credit bureaus, social media platforms, subscription-based organizations and the like all need our personal information. (White, 2019)

When we share our personal information in order to do business with an organization, we trust that they keep our private information private by following it's outlined security protocols.

Our personal information is subject to unauthorized access and theft when an organization fails in delivering on its measures of security. Our personal information becomes subject to unauthorized access and theft.

When you are considering joining an organization and need to give over your personal information, be sure you can trust the organization and its procedures and policies regarding data management and how the data will be used, secured, stored and destroyed before sharing your personal information.

*An Internet connection that's unsecured*—It's really alluring to stop at your local public library, café, or coffee shop and work from your laptop or portable device remotely. It's a good idea to check the Internet connection security that you'll be using before you sign in to their server.

Unsecured or public connections are the most prone to cybercriminals to access your personal data or send malware to your system. It's like inviting hackers into your home when you use unsecured Internet connections.

*Unsecured mobile device*—The warnings also apply to any device that you use to access the Internet— laptops, tablets, smartphones as well as smart home devices like Google Home and Amazon Echo. These devices hold an abundance of private and personal data.

It's imperative to ensure your device is protected from external penetration by maintaining updated firewalls, security and have extra security installed like a two-way authenticator.

The strength of passwords also come under security for your devices. Passwords should include characters, and numbers, as well as letters, should never be the same and never be something easily associated with yourself that can be guessed.

The lack of updated security for your device, even if the Internet connection is secured, is an open invitation for having your data stolen or compromised.

*Scams*—Scams are designed to resemble and feel as authentic as possible, such as a communication you may receive. Robocalls, social engineering, and email phishing methods like personality quizzes are examples of what hackers and cybercriminals have created to steal personal data directly from us and the scams are growing in method and number.

We communicate with brands and people who we trust and we frequently, and mistakenly, trust our communication efforts like phone, social media, and email because these are places that we usually communicate through.

Be aware and vigilant of the type of organizations and how they communicate with the public before your answer. Take a pause and a step back. If you feel uncomfortable, or don't know enough about how an organization communicates, call and ask.

A perfect example of this is the scam calls regarding the IRS. The IRS will never call you or send an email with a link to go to their website and request your personal information. The IRS only sends letters and within their letter is a phone number to call them directly or the website you can go online and log in.

*Data Disposal and Storage at Home*—This is probably one of the most overlooked ways personal data can be compromised. The managing of your data at home.

Are your personal and private documents located in a designated place in your home that is secure and safe? You should have all your personal and private documents stored in one place that only you and other family members know about.

What do you do with information that is no longer needed but yet is sensitive information—such as old bank statements or expired credit cards? If you believe that cutting them up and throwing it out is the answer, your personal data is in jeopardy.

This also goes for old devices like smartphones, laptops, tablet or any other device that stored your personal data. Your personal data can be reconstructed and accessed if you don't destroy the hard drive even after you've disposed of the device. Perhaps you've turned in your laptop to a buy-back program or threw it in the trash which is even worse.

Here is specific information that cybercriminals find valuable. Hackers can use this information to make money by using personal information for fraud, identity theft, duplicating credit cards, and in some instances, even blackmail. The Deep Web marketplace is where the information is readily sold in bulk.

*Properly Destroying and Disposing of Your Data—* We can only protect our personal information from being compromised by a data breach at an organization. If you make yourself aware of the organizations with whom you have a business and are knowledgeable about their policies on data security and data destructions, that's a step in the right direction.

You can have better control of your own data security by taking steps to assess your Internet connections and device security.

Take a step back and think about responding to any telephoned or digital communication. This can help to ensure your private data remains uncompromised and secure.

Purchase a strongbox with a key, or a small safe if necessary, to maintain your private and personal information for your home security

For data disposal, bring your old laptops, tablets, and smartphones to a local data destruction day. These are frequently held at universities. Check with the universities in your area as to when they hold this type of event.

Cybercriminals look for:

- Name

- Date of birth

- Social Security Number

- Email address

- Telephone number

- Physical and/or mailing address

- Clinical information (health provider)

- Bank account number

- Claims information (insurance company or health provider)

If you've become a victim of identity theft or your personal data has been compromised, you should notify your bank. Verify your account and change the password and PIN codes.

Do not download files from sources not known to you or click on suspicious-looking links. Double-check email addresses from emails that you feel don't look quite right or are unfamiliar to you. Even if you receive an email that appears to be from your financial institution, call them and check.

Cybercriminals can ask for credentials posing as bank representatives.

If financials or credentials have been altered, contact the breached company. Ask if they can help to enroll you in a victim assistance program for fraud.

Contact the Federal Trade Commission (FTC) online at IdentityTheft.com or telephone 877-438-4338. (White, 2019)

# Chapter 6: Getting Infected On Legitimate Websites Even Without You Clicking On Anything

Let's face it. Regardless of how careful you are with your devices and the websites you visit, there will be a time when you will unknowingly come up against malware just by downloading a game, a video, or music.

Sometimes, your device can get infected by a cyber-attack that can infect your computer without you doing anything.

How does this happen? There is what's recognized as a Drive-by download attack, and is one that many don't believe can happen. They associate picking up a malware infection as something that only happens by visiting nasty websites they don't frequent.

## How Does a Drive-by Attack Happen?

A common method of spreading malware is the Drive-by attack. Hackers are always on the lookout for websites that are insecure. They embed malevolent script into codes, such as PHP or HTTP on a page on the website.

Someone who visits the website may have malware directly affixed to their computer. The script may directly install malware onto the computer of someone who frequents the site. The victim may be redirected by the hacker to a site they control.

Drive-by attacks don't rely on anyone actively signing into a website to prompt being activated. A drive-by attack operates by embedding code into a web browser or operating system containing flaws in its security due to either lack of updates or unsuccessful updates and takes advantage of these flaws.

You open your laptop one morning, get a cup of coffee and go to a news website that's your favorite. You're on a page, reading about how your football team won and a code that's malicious and embedded into the website, usually what's known as an exploit kit, begins to scan your computer for any vulnerabilities that are not secure.

If your laptop has outdated apps like chat apps, plugins to browsers and more, they can create security holes in your PC.

When a weakness is discovered, the malware infiltrates the system and takes control.

Your first impulse is to blame the owner of the website—that's if you can figure out the source of the infection. But the problem isn't the owner because they probably don't know that their website had malware being distributed to users of the site.

The next thing you'll wonder is why a company that has a large and prominent website would want to allow a malicious agent spreading malware to its users. Unfortunately, this is happening consistently. It's not that they want to have their users' data compromised, but their website has become vulnerable and compromised because of flawed software. Exploit-kit makes hacking fast, easy and profitable.

So, how did your device get an infection from malware without downloading or clicking anything on the website? There are ways that cybercriminals have refined their techniques and tactics and have found different paths to spread their malicious malware.

Attackers compromise websites with malicious elements embedded inside in drive-by download attacks. The range of this malware includes malvertisements, cross-site scripting attacks known as XSS, malicious redirects to malicious

JavaScript code injects, malicious iFrames executing obscurely or other sly attack methods that a user can't catch on their own.

Regardless of the tactic, it is very clear what the objectives are of cybercriminals. They want to either steal your financial or identity information or run malicious software on your computer.

The result of your device being compromised ranges from adware infections to data encryption with a ransomware infection or financial loss.

## You're Exposing Your Device to Drive-by Attacks

You don't want to be the victim of a cyber-attack, but you may be leaving yourself open to one, albeit unintentionally.

Some of the ways you're leaving yourself vulnerable and practically opening the door to cybercriminals with a "Welcome" sign are:

*Your software isn't updated*—This means your operating system, browsers, plugin, browsers, apps, mobile apps and more.

If you think that it's no problem with your devices not being updated, think again. There have been approximately 1,004 vulnerabilities a year since 2016 that the top three browsers most commonly used have had.

This means that the attacker takes full control over the compromised system that has this many security issues. After that, the hacker can do whatever they want.

You probably won't see the drive-by download coming either. Not when you're reading your favorite news website.

*Hoarding plugins and add-ons in your browsers*—The more plug-ins and add-ons you have installed in your browsers, the greater the likelihood that one of them will be hacked.

These may make your life easier, but it's also giving entrée to all types of developers to your browser. Not a great idea.

If you haven't taken a look to see what's going on with plug-ins in your browser, it may be a good time to take a look.

https://www.google.com/search?q=how+do+you +check+for+plug- ins+on+your+computer&rlz=1C1GGRV

*You're not using a safe browser when shopping or banking online*—Drive-by download attacks are always looking for the entry point of browsers. If you're always using Internet Explorer for all the Internet-related activities, this can be a problem, especially if you're what the previous reason points out—a digital hoarder.

If you want to solve this problem, admit you've hoarded. We all do it at some time until we get smart.

Financial data and any identifying information are what make cybercriminals swoon. Take care of your browser and send them packing.

*You're using a free antivirus for all your online protection*—You have probably heard this before, and it just doesn't seem to sink in—Your antivirus cannot provide the ability to know and block every threat that is out there in cyberspace. And only one security product isn't enough.

Software and hardware are too complicated. Cybercrimes come along in such vast numbers that no one company could possibly handle them alone. The companies that manufacture security products are realistic about what they can offer a user by way of securing their system.

It would be great for one security product to be the one that keeps our data safe and uncompromised. Working to have that become more likely is better than wasting time wishing it was.

## What Malware Can Do

Most people don't realize what malware can do. It can wreak havoc on devices by being bundled together.

There are malicious software cocktails such as *Fileless* malware which even your antivirus would not be able to detect. Aptly named, this infection doesn't use any files and runs in the RAM memory of your device.

These Drive-by attacks are infamously crafty. Using the *Fileless* malware adds to the method and enhances the impact.

Your smartphones and tablets aren't safe—Most people think that by default, their mobile devices are safe from a malware attack. Androids are afflicted by Drive-by downloads and all types of malware. The attacks are included on the menu as well. And you probably have more information on your phone than our PCs.

You use your phone for EVERYTHING! It knows who you've spoken with, what messages you've sent, you do your online banking, purchases at Starbucks, you listen to music, play games, and more on your phone... Why do you leave it unprotected?

You need to update your operating system, otherwise, the opportunities you give to hackers to attack will multiply.

People think that products by Apple can't be hacked! Although Apple products and their operating systems are more secure than many others, they are still prone to be maliciously hacked.

There was on the Drive-by case of an attacking that involved a website that you could download to be connected to the Dalai Lama which specifically targeted Mac users.

It's not wise to take unnecessary risks when another download can create havoc on your Mac or smartphone.

## Protect Your Devices and Data from Drive-by Attacks

There is more that you can do to keep your sensitive information sheltered and away from the malicious and greedy hands of online criminals.

*Update your software as soon as it's ready*—Your software maker releases updates and as soon as they do, cybercriminals are at the ready to reverse engineer it and seek out users on the Internet who haven't applied the update.

This is the reason for updating your software and your operating system is major and why you need to do it quickly.

Updates can be easily automated. Some software updates automatically if you prompt it to do so. Once the software is updated, it's time to go to the next step.

*Your software needs to be cleaned up*—The more exposed you are with the more plug-ins you have.

Declutter those plugins! Only keep the products you use and trust constantly. You will feel much safer and be safer. Another plus is your PC speed will get an extra boost.

*Use separate browsers*—Use a separate browser for your financial and retail activity. These are activities where you expose your bank account and credit card information. Continuing to use the same browser for all your activities on the Internet just leaves you open for a possible attack.

Although it's possible for Chrome, Internet Explorer, and Chrome to be formulated for security and privacy with plugins, there are some other browsers that can be used.

They are minus all the platforms and plugins, and all non-essential features to create a minimalist experience. (Techworld Staff, 2018)

- Firefox

- Waterfox

- Pale Moon

- HTTPS Everywhere

- Tor

*Use a reliable antivirus*—It's an important step to choose the best antivirus for your PC. Compare the antivirus protection and make sure it has a built-in URL checker.

*Let's Review*—To have protection from Drive-by attacks, stay with sites you usually use. Don't be too complacent about these websites. They can be vulnerable and can be attacked.

Eliminate unnecessary apps. Let's repeat this warning one more time—the more plugins, the greater the vulnerabilities that can be used for Drive-by attacks.

Protect all your devices. Their security shouldn't be taken for granted. Don't ignore your tablet or phone... even your smart TV.

Just as the security of devices is improving, so too malware creators will improve their Drive-by attacks.

You need to have security as a central element of your digital devices and life. Security is not a "maybe-I'll-get it-later" thing, it's an, "I need it right away thing."

Forewarned is forearmed.

# Chapter 7: 3 Insidious Password Security Attacks And How To Avoid Them

Our password is the entrée into all our devices, browsers and websites. The password is for our security. We've all been warned about never sharing a password, or never using passwords that are too easy to hack like Bill2000 or Password123.

We use a password to get into our business' computer system, our health provider's website, our bank's website. Regardless of the industry, there are password rules that are being enforced because of password security.

We've read about the security breach disasters like Equifax credit reporting company's breach of security that compromised the social security numbers of its members, or Target, the major retailer whose breach gave access to customer's credit card information.

Adhering to an employers' password security instructions are what most people do, yet many still question why these passwords guidelines are even effective. Some people don't understand how a more complicated, longer password using letters (some capitalized), numbers, etc. could possibly make a difference. They make it so complicated that no one could ever guess the password.

This is a major mindset that needs to be changed. Hackers are in the business of attaining financial information—this is their job and what they do. When you understand how they do this, it will give the answer as to why passwords that are complicated and security with advanced methods, such as authentication that is multi-factored, are so crucial.

There are three password attacks are the most commonly used to hack into systems that are protected by passwords:

*Brute Force attack*—A hacker uses a script or computer program to try logging in with combinations of possible passwords.

They usually begin by guessing the easiest passwords. For example, if the hacker was able to retrieve a company's list of names, if even one of the employees has an easy password like Bill2000 or Password123, he'll be able to get in.

This is the easiest attack for a hacker to execute and one of the most common forms of password attacks. These attacks don't begin at random. They start with the easiest-to-guess passwords. (Kaseya, 2018)

*Dictionary attack*—The opposite of a brute force attack is the dictionary attack. This attack has hackers employing a program that cycles through words that are common. While the brute force attack proceeds letter by letter, a dictionary attack only attempts to find the possibilities that have the potential to be successful.

Some key factors of a users' psychology are what dictionary attacks depend on. For example, many users base their passwords off common words and are apt to choose short passwords.

Dictionary attacks begin with the words and variations of those words, adding numbers, transposing letters with numbers, etc. (Canner, 2019)

Dictionary attacks are successful because most people lean in the direction of choosing passwords which are 7 characters or less, using single words found in dictionaries or predictable variations on words that are simple. (Kaseya, 2018)

*Key Logger attack*—Hackers use a program to track a user's keystrokes so by the end of a day of tracking all the information the user has typed, including passwords and IDs, the keystrokes have been recorded.

This is different than a dictionary or brute force attack in numerous ways. The keylogging program that's used is a malware or full-blown virus. The malware or virus must first penetrate the user's device which is accomplished by tricking the user into downloading it, often by sending an email with a link to click on.

Key logger attacks also differ because there isn't much protection for stronger passwords. This is one of the reasons multi-factor authentication (MFA) has become a must for all organizations and businesses.

A user is required to gain access to the system by using the two-factor authentication (2FA, an advanced authentication, also known as multi-factor authentication). They need to provide not only a password but another security factor, such as an exclusive, one-time access code generated from a token device or secure mobile app on their smartphone is needed to gain access.

Networks protected by MFA are almost impossible to penetrate through an outside attack. A hacker won't be able to provide the second security factor even if they are able to hack in and get the system password.

Google, Paypal, Facebook, and others all offer MFA options. It is growing quickly as the systems' security method of choice. Many industries and agencies including the FBI, HIPPA, and PCI require MFA for anyone attempting to log into their systems offsite according to their security guidelines. (Kaseya, 2018)

## Other Types of Attacks

Brute Force, Dictionary, and Key Logger attack plague individuals and companies who use their passwords to log into websites and company systems. There are other attack types that have been used and may not be as popular with hackers as they used to be, but are still being used to gain access and information.

*Rainbow Table Attack*—This attack is a bit complex and takes some understanding of the technical aspects of this type of attack.

Companies often do what's known as "hashing" their users' passwords. Hashing mathematically converts caches of passwords. They appear to be random strings of characters, preventing them from being misused. They can't be abused if hackers can't read the passwords.

Although hashing seems to sound like a strong security method to protect the identity and all other data, that isn't quite the story. It can mean the difference between a worrying but fixable problem versus a breach that can ruin a company's reputation. However, in looking at this method, it may not always work.

For example, a list of pre-computed hashes is compiled by a round table. It already has possible password combinations for hash algorithms via the mathematical answers. This one uses the time to its advantage.

*Password Spraying*—This attack is a member of the Brute Force password attack family. Password spraying attempts to try thousands, or millions of accounts simultaneously with some passwords that are commonly used. If even one user's password is weak, a company's business may be put at risk.

While Brute Force attacks target a single account, password spraying increases the targets exponentially and helps hackers side-step lockout policies on accounts that could generate repeat login failure.

Hackers like to attack consistently from one account to the next applying different passwords to see if they work. The attack methods seem to move slowly.

Password spraying can be especially dangerous for cloud-based authentication portals or single-sign-on accounts.

*Traffic Interception*—This attack has the cybercriminal Packet Sniffer software to check network traffic, capturing passwords as they are passed.

The software checks and captures information that's critical, similar to tapping a phone line or eavesdropping. The work is easier if the passwords are unencrypted and, depending on the strength of the encryption method used, encrypted information may be easily decryptable and compromised.

*Baiting*—Attackers leave USBs or other devices that are infected in the employer or public locations hoping people will pick them up and used it.

*Quid Quo Pro*—Cybercriminals impersonate someone such as a help desk employee and engage with a user that requires obtaining information from them.

*Credential Stuffing*—In all the other password attack techniques, it is assumed that hackers have yet to secure users' passwords. This may not be true. One of the least reported yet disastrous effects of any data breach is the ripple effect on other enterprises. In the long term, data breaches essentially lead to other breaches.

This principle is demonstrated by credential stuffing. Hackers use lists of stolen passwords and user names in combination with numerous accounts. It automatically tries again and again until a match is hit.

Users using the same password for several accounts is what credential stuffing counts on, and is frequently very successful. Additionally, stolen passwords on the Dark Web being shared or being sold to them means the information multiplies among threat actors.

This attack falls under the Brute Force password attack techniques. It proves to be extremely effective because the passwords are already known.

## How to Prevent Password Attacks

Using a strong password against a password attack is the first defense. Using easy to remember yet hard to guess passwords is endorsed. A good mix of upper and lowercase characters, special characters, and numbers helps.

Avoiding the use of common words or phrases is a way to prevent being hacked. Don't use specific words for any of the sites you visit. This includes the app you're logging into.

It is recommended checking any passwords against a dictionary of poor passwords that are known.

Not depending on only one password is another recommendation by the National Institute of Standards and Technology (NIST). Companies specifically should use single sign-on (SSO) and MFA.

It's important to educate employees. Teach employees the methods hackers use and how they can be aware and recognize them.

On your own personal devices, change your passwords, especially those that lead to websites that have personal and private data such as your bank, credit card companies, and retail sites as well as your sign on to your devices.

## Some Password Protection Advice

You should be using a password manager. This is imperative, along with two-factor authentication. This will keep your data safe. (Cunningham, 2019)

Using the word "password" as your password or your birthday or your pet's name you probably already know is not a good idea.

However, even worse than using these as passwords is using the same password across many of the sites you log into. This is something that more than 50% of people are doing.

Hackers can easily use that password to get into all your other accounts, even if only one of these accounts is compromised.

Although you may resist at first and continue reusing the same passwords for all your sites because it's too hard to create strong, unique passwords and remember which password goes to what website, you need to use a password manager.

Even if you are using two-factor authentication and keeping your computer's operating system and web browser updated, it's the most important thing to protect yourself and your privacy online.

A password manager can replace the little pad or bits of paper that you may have scribbled down all your passwords. It is an automated, all-digital, secure place to have those passwords recorded and remembered.

Strong new passwords are generated when you change a password or create a new account that needs a login. It stores all your passwords all in one place and, in some cases, your bank accounts, addresses, credit card numbers, and other information.

All your information is protected by a master password. The password manager remembers all the other information. Whenever you log in to a site or app, the program manager fills in the username and password.

Google's Smart Lock generates, saves, and auto-fills passwords in Chrome and Android or in Safari and iOS, Apple's Keychain, but a good password manager does more.

Password managers can alert you proactively to when a password is being reused if your passwords are easy to guess or hack, and weak. Some password managers will alert you to when an account has been hacked online and your passwords are compromised and exposed.

If you're sharing accounts with family members, friends, or even co-workers, there are password managers that offer family plans making it simple to share complex, strong passwords without needing a myriad of people to write them down or remember them.

Using a password manager can seem intimidating, but when you begin to use one and begin to create strong and random passwords, you'll wonder how you lived without one.

Some password managers are:

- 1Password—reasonable fee based
- LastPassFree—free
- Dashlane—fee-based

Compare each product and choose which one is right for you and/or your family. (Cunningham, 2019)

# Chapter 8: Bypassing Security Systems By Tricking The Back End

## What is an SQLi Attack?

An SQLi attack, also known as an SQL injection attack is where application security measures can be bypassed on the web, allowing attackers to use SQL injection vulnerabilities.

Attackers have the ability to get hold of the total database by going around authentication and the permission of an application. They can also modify, add, and erase records.

SQL Injection vulnerability can affect any users of an SQL database. Gaining unapproved entrée to customer information, trade secrets and the like is the reason cybercriminals may use it.

SQL Injection impact on a business is sweeping. The unauthorized viewing of user lists, the possibility of an attacker gaining a databases' administrative rights, and totally deleting tables are among those things considered to be a successful SQL Injection attack. (Imperva.com, 2019)

The additional cost of an SQLi attack is the possible loss of trust by the customer if their addresses, phone numbers their credit card information are stolen.

## SQL Queries

To achieve entrée to databases for manipulation and create customized views, SQL language is used. It executes orders for updates, the removal of records and recovery of data.

### How is This Attack Executed?

In order to make an SQL Injection attack, a vulnerable user input on the web page or web application must be found by an attacker. A web application is sent by the attacker, and malicious SQL orders are implemented.

The SQL query is calculated to oversee information stowed in interpersonal databases. It's used to modify, retrieve and erase data where websites applications have data stored.

Consequently, there can be very serious consequences if an SQL Injection attack is successful.

Identifications of other users in the database can be found by the attacker using SQL injection. The attacker can mimic these users. The mimicked user may have all database privileges as a database administrator.

Output data from the database can be selected by SQL. An SQLi gives an attacker the ability to have entrée to complete data.

Data in a database can be altered by SQL and new data can be added. For example, in an application that's financial, an attacker can void transactions, transfer money to their account, or alter balances.

Even if there are database backups made by the administrator, data that is deleted could affect the availability of the application until the database is restored. Additionally, the most recent data may not be the most recent backup data.

## Rasputin Attacks

An alleged lone hacker, identified as Rasputin, successfully breached dozens of universities and government agencies' databases. The attack began in late 2016 and continued into 2017.

The hacker was said to have used SQL injection attacks against web applications of the victims and tried to sell access to the databases.

The victims attacked:

- University of Cambridge

- Cornell University

- S. Department of Housing and Urban Development

- S. Post Regulatory Commission

- Rhode Island Department of Education

And many more...

SQLi attacks find web applications and inject commands to the database. They can modify and/or disclose information kept in the application's database. (Calyptix, 2017)

The most common SQL injection examples include:

- Retrieving hidden data, and modifying an SQL query to return more results.

- Destabilizing application logic where a query can be changed to hamper the application's logic.

- UNION attacks where different database tables can have their data taken from them.

*The Types of SQL Injections Attacks*

There are three categories of SQL injections:

- In-band SQLi (classical)
- Inferential SQLi (blind)
- Out-of-band SQLi

*In-band SQLi*—The same channel of communications is used by the attacker to launch their attacks and collect their results. The efficiency and simplicity of this type of SQLi attack make it one of the most common types used.

In-band SQLi has two sub-variations:

*Error-based SQLi*—The database produces messages that can be collected by the attacker for knowledge of the databases' construction.

*Union-based SQLi*—This combines several statements that are created to attain a response. This may have information that the attacker uses for leverage.

*Inferential SQLi*—This is the blind SQL that is usually slower to execute because the injections depend on the behavioral patterns and response of the server, but can be damaging. Blind SQL injections are classified as:

*Out-of-band SQLi*—When a server is unstable or slow or a channel to start an attack is unusable, the out-of-band SQLi is performed.

The server to transmit information is what these techniques count on.

*Dictionary attack*—A dictionary attack is a technique of breaking into a computer or a server that is protected by a password by methodically entering every word in a dictionary as a password.

Another reason the Dictionary attack is used is to find the key that's necessary to attack an encrypted document or message and decrypt it.

The Dictionary attack works because businesses and computer users continue to use ordinary words as passwords. When a system employs multiple-word phrases and random combinations of numerals with letters of upper and lower case, a dictionary attack is rarely successful. (Ostrowick, 2019)

*Key Logger attack*—Keylogging, also known as keystroke logging or keyboard, usually secretly, so the person using the keyboard does not know their typing action is being observed.

Software or hardware is designed to steal passwords or other sensitive information by recording keyboard entries. It can also be a small device connected to a keyboard or PC.

The data that can be stolen by a key logger attack:

- Passwords

- Login Identification

- CC/DB Number and Verification Code

- Entire Chat History

- Entire Search History

- Screenshots of the activity on a computer

- Details of Opened and Worked on documents

*How to Avert a SQL Injection*

A firewall is usually used to filter out SQLi and other dangers. A firewall usually depends on a constantly updated list of fastidiously made signs that will extract surgically SQL queries.

This type of list has signs that deal with particular directions for an attack, patched frequently to presenting procedures to block any weaknesses that are newly discovered. (Imperva.com, 2019)

# Chapter 9: Attacking Through the Weakest Link in the Chain

The XSS vulnerability has been one of the most critical web application security risks released that has been on every OWASP Top 10 list.

### Cross-Site Definition

Cross-site Scripting, also known as XSS, bypasses the Same Origin Policy (SOP) in a susceptible web application.

XSS attacks employ source matter in a victim's browser third-party web resources in the victim's web browser to run scripts.

When user input is not clean whenever HTML code is created and is reproduced, an attacker can embed his own code. The browser will continue to reflect the user's code because it relates to the website.

An attacker can then inject code very easily, which would run under the context of the site. An attacker has the ability to open other pages on the domain, and by doing so, reads the set cookies or data such as CSRF-tokens.

User accounts may be damaged, Trojan horse programs can be activated, and content modified depending on the harshness of the attack.

*Types of XSS Vulnerability*

*Stored Cross-Site Scripting Vulnerability*—Stored XSS vulnerabilities occur when the payload is kept in a database and then implemented.

Stored Cross-site scripting is hazardous due to:

- The browser's XSS filter does not reveal the payload; it's not visible.

- Users may trigger the payload by accident if the affected page is visited while a specific form or crafted URL input is needed for misusing reproduced XSS.

- XSS that is stored can be very hazardous, particularly when exploited on popular pages since it can the effect of the worm.

*Reflected XSS*—When unstored data is reproduced on the page, malicious content can be taken and injected, sending a fashioned URL or post that is malicious to the user. If the user clicks on the link, the payload will be implanted.

Browsers like Chrome, Internet Explorer or Edge are generally being caught with this kind of payload by built-in XSS filters.

*For example*: Use a news website and their search functionality. The website reflects the query that was searched for.

The results of the search the website reflects the content of the query that the user searched for. If the functionality of the Search on the website is susceptible to a reflected XSS, a malicious URL will be sent to a user by the attacker.

When the user clicks on the URL that's malicious, the XSS attack is executed. The website displays the code, a reflection of the code, redirecting the user's browser. The attacker is now in control and then steals the tokens/session cookies from the browser.

*DOM Based Cross-site Scripting Vulnerability—* The vulnerability occurs in the Document Object Model (DOM) rather than part of the HTML.

In stored and reflective Cross-site scripting attacks the vulnerability payload can be seen in the response page. In the DOM-based cross-site scripting, the response of the attack and the HTML source code will be exactly the same, that is, the payload can't be found in the response. It can only be seen by investigating the DOM of the page or on runtime.

*Impact of Cross-site Scripting*—The impact of XSS vulnerability varies on web applications. It spans from user's Session Hijacking and, if used along with a social engineering attack, it can also head to the disclosure of data that is sensitive in nature, CSRF attack, and vulnerabilities of other security.

An attacker who exploits an XSS vulnerability can mimic the user and overtake the user's account. Even worse, if administrative rights are held by the user, execution of the code may be implemented on the server.

*Averting XSS Vulnerabilities*—It may be enough, in some cases, to encode with opening and closing tags as the HTML special characters. In other situations, it is necessary to correctly apply URL encoding.

Don't allow any link that is not is whitelisted and doesn't begin such as https:// or http://. This will prevent the use of URI schemes, like javascript://

Although web browsers now have an XSS filter built-in, sanitation is what is needed to diminish the effect of any vulnerabilities that exist. An XSS filter is secondary in defending from attacks. (Netsparker Security Team, 2019)

# Chapter 10: Snooping In Weak Client-Server Communications

Snooping and eavesdropping. These are two activities that some people do—just because. Some people have the need to know everything that's going on, even if it doesn't concern them.

Sometimes kids snoop in places they shouldn't, their curiosity, natural in most children, is piqued and they look to satisfy their need to know.

These activities, in some ways innocent (when it comes to kids), can be annoying. In the context of security, snooping is having access to another company's or person's data although they're unauthorized to have that access and secrete it illegally.

This type of snooping is more than annoying; it's dangerous to your personal and private information.

## What is Snooping?

Snooping is similar to eavesdropping, but getting access to data while it's being transmitted is not necessarily limited. Snooping can include watching what someone else is typing or casually walking by a computer and observing an email that appears on someone else's computer screen.

Snooping that's more sophisticated scans a computer using software programs and remotely watches the activity on that computer or network device.

Corporations occasionally legitimately check-in (quietly) on their employees. They observe how they use their computers and follow their use of their business computers and their use of the Internet. Governments may want to collect information and avert terrorism and crime so they snoop on individuals to achieve this.

Keyloggers maliciously hack to monitor keystrokes gain passwords and seize private communications, emails and data transmissions.

Snooping is generally thought of as having a negative overtone. Snooping can be attributed to computer technology to any utility or program that monitors activity. For example, network traffic is captured for analysis on a snoop server. The snooping protocol checks on a computer to make sure there is capable processing. (Rouse, 2019)

There are several kinds of information that result in the loss of privacy because of snooping in network security. They may be one or all of these types of information:

- Passwords

- Private data

- Low-level Internet information

- Financial details

## Eavesdropping Attack

An attack is when someone attempts to steal information transmitted on a network by computers, smartphones, or other devices. With networks that are unsecured, communication is taken advantage of to have access to data being sent and received.

Network transmissions do not appear to be operating abnormally, making the detection of an eavesdropping attack to be difficult to detect.

*How an Eavesdropping Attack Works*

A connection between a client and server is weakened, letting the attacker have traffic on the network sent to itself. There can be software that monitors a network, installing a sniffer on a server or computer, to execute an attack and seize information that's transmitted.

A point of weakness are devices that transmit data between the receiver device getting the transmission in the network.

*Active and Passive Eavesdropping—What's the Difference?*

Passive and Active attacks differ in the active attacker intercepts the information and modifies it. The passive attacker doesn't modify the intercepted information that is transmitted but analyzes and reads the data. (Techdifferences.com, 2018)

These are the two basic definitions and differences between an active and passive attack. However, there is more to their differences.

Aside from the fact that the active attack modifies the information, it also always causes damage to the system. Passive attacks don't harm the system.

The threat to the availability and integrity of the transmitted information is what occurs in an active attack, while the threat of the passive attack is the confidentiality of information is compromised.

The victim of an active attack is made aware that the attack took place, while a passive attack does not alert the victim.

The transmission is physically controlled in an active attack, while the passive attack only observes the information transmitted.

*Active Eavesdropping*

An active attack has the attacker seize the connection and revise the
information. The attacker has an active hand in changing the information that is being transmitted.

The active attack is difficult to prevent. There is a vast range of possible physical, software and network vulnerabilities. Rather than prevention, it highlights on the revelation of recovery from any delay or disruption that is caused by it.

This attack creates a huge amount of damage to the system.

This type of eavesdropping needs more effort and frequently has more risky implications. The victim becomes aware of an attack when the hacker tries to execute it.

*Active Attacks are Interruption, Modification, and Fabrication*

*Interruption*—An attacker who is unauthorized to have access to a transmission attempts to pose as another entity. This attack is also known as a Masquerade Attack.

*Modification*—Replay attack and alteration are two ways that modifying of the data can be accomplished. The replay attack captures some data units or a sequence of events and resends it. The message being altered has some changes made to the original transmission, either can cause a change to the message.

*Fabrication*—This part of the active attack causes DoS attacks. It seeks to thwart users who are authorized from being able to access some services which they are allowed to access.

In other words, the authorized user is locked out after the attacker gains control of the network.

## Passive Eavesdropping

Eavesdropping has always been a security problem. An attacker listens to network transmissions passively to have access to information that's private, like routing updates, node identification numbers, or application of sensitive information.

This type of attack is difficult to detect because the data or system resources are not altered in any way. The attacker is just gathering information or monitoring the transmission. There is no change or alteration to the system or the data.

The victim of a passive attack is not alerted about the attack as in an active attack. They don't have a clue.

The data can be encrypted and encoded in unintelligible language by the sender and converted to understandable language by the receiver is a way a passive attack can be prevented.

During the transmission, the transmission is formed in an incomprehensible code that can't be deciphered or understood by the hackers. Prevention of a passive attack is more of a concern than detecting that an attack is underway.

Open ports not protected by firewalls cause passive attacks. Once the continuous search for vulnerabilities is found, the attacker has access to the system and network.

There are two types of passive attacks:

*Message content is release*—A sender wishes to send a message that is confidential or an email to the receiver. The contents of the message are what the sender doesn't want someone other than the receiver to read.

*Analysis of traffic*—Messages can be disguised to have information extracted by using encryption. However, the pattern can be watched and the traffic analyzed to extract information.

*Ways to Protect Your Emails and Confidential Information*

One way to protect against eavesdropping attacks is to know what software is installed in devices connected to a network.

Other ways are avoiding public networks, such as your favorite café or coffee hangout, or the library, particularly for transactions that are sensitive.

Using personal firewalls, virtual private networks (VPN) and updated antivirus software that can deter eavesdropping attacks as well. (Techdifferences.com, 2018)

Eavesdropping attacks target public Wi-Fi networks because they make easy targets. Anyone using one of these networks and has a password that is easily available can oversee the activity using free software by enrolling in the network.

They can steal valuable login credentials and data that are transmitted over the network by users.

Phones should have an up-to-date version and have it running to sometimes limit the user being subject to an eavesdropping attack.

However, phone vendors do not always make the latest version available and users have no access or way to have it downloaded until the vendor releases it. (Techdifferences.com, 2018)

## A Few Ways to Avoid Leaving Tracks on the Internet

Your information is collected when you go on Google or Facebook and then that data is sold to advertisers. Websites have invisible "cookies" that are deposited onto our computers. They record where we go online. Our own government has been known to track what sites we visit and where we go online. (Pogue, 2019)

You could do all the suggested remedies like using a password program and make every password different. Or, have an ad blocker installed in your web browser like uBlock Origin for example. If you're on Facebook, have the Privacy Settings be limited in the ads that are targeted to you. And don't pass up any articles that tell about the latest Internet scam or virus.

*Google*

These ideas have merit, but it's other ideas that you should consider. One is to discontinue using Google as your mailing service and search engine for the web. Any of the Google services such as Google Maps, Google Docs, etc.

Google knows more about you than any other system. If you want to be protected and not have your every Internet move or search tracked, then using a web search engine like DuckDuckGo is probably a choice to consider.

DuckDuckGo's search results are frequently not as useful as Google's, but it is advertised to not track your searches or you.

If you want to lessen the incentive of anyone trying to look at your emails and preserve your privacy, paying for your email account may be the solution.

ProtonMail costs $4 per month, has privacy features including end-to-end encryption and anonymous sign-up.

## Avoid Web Tracking That's Unnecessary

If you get creeped out by the tracking that brings targeted ads for you, try Ghostery, a free plug-in for web browsers who want to block trackers and lists them by category.

## Don't Use Facebook to Sign In

Never register on a new website using the Facebook sign-in shortcut or the Google sign in shortcut. It allows those companies to track where you go on other sites.

For those of you who love shortcuts and speediness, it's safer to register the long way with an email address and password. (Pogue, 2019)

# Chapter 11: Brute Force Assaults Using A Weird Mathematical Paradox

Behind figures, there's an underlying logic, although it doesn't often seem to be anything logical, that an obvious situation or conclusion that appears on the surface seems not to be the conclusion.

A disconnect between science and logic tumbles spills into the world, serious consequences could be the result. An example of this is the Birthday Paradox.

## The Birthday Paradox

There need to be 253 people in the room for there to be a 50% probability that someone in the same room with you shares the same birthday as you.

*HOWEVER*, in order for there to be a probability of 50% or more than two people in the same room share the same birthday, you only need 23 people to be in the room.

*Underlying Theory of the Birthday Paradox*

The answer to the paradox lies in a theory of probability and number matching principles.

*Birthday Paradox*—The theory of probability involves a chance that in a group of people who are chosen randomly, a pair of them share the same birthday.

If there are 367 people in the room, the likelihood is set 100% since in a standard leap year (365 or 366 days) there are only 366 possible birthdays. This is set by the 'pigeonhole principle' of probability.

These probabilities or likelihoods are the outcomes of simple third-party number matching: It's like an outside viewer is looking over all the numbers to locate matching pairs.

Supposing that every day of the year, (except February 29th), is equally probable as the date of birth, there's a 99.9% likelihood a match is viewed with a group of 70 people and a 50% probability with 23.

The viewpoint of somebody in the first person, scanning through the room to find someone with a matching birthday to their own birthday, and the state of affairs goes paradoxical, necessitating there to be 253 people in the room.
(Finjan Team, 2017)

This occurs because pairs are the basis of the birthday matches—it would take 253 pairings to get a 50% likelihood of matching to a single (first person's) birthday.

But, if every person in the room is permitted to connect with every other person to find a matching pair (without the limitation of the single birthday) the number of people needed in the room to realize 50% likelihood falls to 23.

*Collision Problem and Hash Function*—Hash functions are mathematical processes in cryptography that are used to diminish larger strings of data into strings that are fixed in length and smaller (also known as keys or hash values) that represent the larger string.

An ideal encryption scenario is the value is unique for each hash and when the hash is decrypted, the one specific string which produced it can be traced back.

However, very large data sets may have encryption put on over it, and the possibility exists a given hash function that two diverse inputs may be hashed down to the value of the same output.

When this happens, it is known as collision and may have security implications. This replication in hash values is also known as fingerprints, checksums, or digests.

*Birthday Attack*—A birthday attack abuses communication between two or more parties. It is a kind of attack that is cryptographic and exploits the math probability theory behind the birthday.

The attempts between a random attack and a fixed degree of permutations are how the success of this attack determines the likelihood of collisions.

*Example*—A classroom of a teacher and 30 students. The teacher wants to find pairs of students that have the same birthday. The teach requests for the students' birthdays to find a pair. Naturally, this value may appear small. For instance, if the teacher sets a specific date of October 4th, the probability that at least one student is born on that day is $1-(364/365)^{30}$ which is approximately 7.9%.

However, at least one student would have the October 4th birthday like any other student in the class is around 70% is the probability (Sant, 2019)

*The vulnerability of digital signatures*—By computing a cryptographic function a message can be digitally signed, under normal conditions, with an associated secret key signing it.

However, two versions of a message can be created by an attacker. One message has been changed but looks legitimate with (as an example) additional commas, spaces to make it to a specific size or blank lines, and a (false) message that is padded out as well. (Finjan Team, 2017)

A digital signature's hash function, (easy with correct computing power and software), may be applied to both the legitimate and false documents until they return the same hash value.

Any number of scams that involve having recipients to sign either form of the document, and/or document switching may eventually follow.

*Counter-Remedies*—To prevent a birthday attack, mathematical protection can be done by making the hash output length function for a digital signature so big it becomes impractical for the attacker to perform a Brute Force birthday assault.

Normally, twice as many bits would be necessary to prevent a Brute Force attack.

Some measure of protection may also be provided by the person signing a document by making changes that are random, like integrating spaces and commas, as an example. These changes don't alter the form of the message overall and retain a personal record of the changes and a copy as proof of both their own signature and the changes. (Finjan Team, 2017)

# Chapter 12: Making Sense of Malware Software

Malware. We know it's bad for our computer or mobile devices, and that it can infect a network or a system, but what exactly is malware?

We all, individuals and businesses, should be consistently concerned with the threats we face online. Malware threatens everyone and those who are worried about online security and safety should know as much about malware threats as possible, as well as their classifications and ways to protect yourself.

## What is Malware?

Software that is designed to enable unauthorized access or to damage computer systems is malware.

These are pieces of software that are dangerous, usually, come in the shape of code or files, and execute actions and corrupt or destroy files that are stored within your network or on your computer.

Malware is typically used to take control of a device on the receiving end of transmission and data, for spamming individuals who are unsuspecting, or for stealing data. The use of malware can be for destructive purposes from stealing personal information such as financial or credit card information to destroying a company's entire network, compromising not only the company's data but the data of their clients as well.

The amount of information that is housed on the Internet has increased exponentially and so has the amount of possible damage these programs can cause as well.

There is much to gain by the creators and distributors of Malware software. The growth of these programs mirrors the growth of the benign software market.

Much of the reason malware is used by hackers is for financial gain as well as the aspiration to wreak havoc and destruction. The major motivating factor for most of the hackers and creators of malware is money. This is evidenced by the final goal of why malware is used—for theft. It could be the theft of data, ransom, or the plain old theft of money.

There are many shapes and sizes that malware comes in, but regardless of the difference in appearance, it all has the same purpose and that is being disruptive to computer systems. This may be to stealing information, damaging files, or creating numerous issues with the functionality of a computer.

Since the creation of computers, malicious programs have come into existence. The first virus to appear was written in the early 1970s and was known as the "*Creeper Worm*".

The Creeper Worm was a self-replicating program and designed to duplicate itself on other systems. It displayed a message which was harmless. Although there was no malignant intent from the Creeper Worm, the ones that followed were not.

These viruses cemented their place in the digital world. The form of viruses carried from one computer to the next and injected on floppy disks via code was the earliest malware.

Viruses now travel at Internet speed which has improved the method of transmission. As anti-malware programs have been advanced by technology, malware has kept up by becoming more refined.

Studies executed by online security companies have discovered that hackers stole $172 billion from people in 2017 worldwide. The main method used to steal was malware.

Malware as a business can be extremely lucrative; this is why there have been a number of malicious programs that have mushroomed and come to the fore in the past few years.

*The Melissa Virus*

There are many examples of malware attacks that have been executed since the late 1990s. Although the following example may be antiquated by today's more sophisticated and intricate malware of today, this demonstrates how destructive a malware virus can be.

The Melissa virus posed as a Word file that contained passwords to adult sites. Anyone who was curious opened the document which then executed a macro that resent the virus to the address book of the first 50 people in each user's contact list.

Emails that resulted from this virus hit corporations, including Intel and Microsoft, and governments. In its entirety, the financial damage that resulted from this one virus was $1.1 billion dollars.

The creator of the malware, David L. Smith had been sentenced to ten years, but after helping the FBI to hunt down other virus creators, he was released after 20 months. (It Pro, 2017)

*Zeus*

First discovered in July 2007, this Trojan Horse was used to steal data from the United States Department of Transportation.

Two years later 74,000 FTP accounts from banks to corporations including Amazon, Cisco, and Bank of America had been compromised. Using a Man-in-Browser keystroke logging, this Zeus botnet, the largest on the Internet to date, had been set up to swipe the details of login for bank and email accounts and social networks.

More than 1 million computers were attacked and infected and $70 million was stolen by the Zeus cyber theft ring. An Algerian hacker, Hamza Bendelladj, was the alleged creator and orchestrator of this malware and sentenced in 2016 to 15 years in prison. (It Pro, 2017)

## *WannaCry*

This was the largest malware attack in history. When this malware was let loose in May 2017, WannaCry infected more than 300,000 computers in 150 countries. This ransomware crypto worm targeted computers running the Windows operating system.

The reason the ransomware was able to be unleashed was the older versions of Windows had a security vulnerability. Although Microsoft had issued patches for this vulnerability, there were those organizations that had not applied them.

The National Health Service (NHS) was the primary victim and saw 70,000 devices affected including computers, MRI scanners, and refrigerators programmed to specific temperature control to store blood.

The WannaCry attack cost the NHS over $100,000,000. Marcus Hutchins, a
25-year old from England was the creator of the malware. Although he helped to shut down the attack on the NHS, he was arrested by the FBI in Las Vegas months later after he had attended a hacking convention.

U.S. District Judge Joseph Peter Stadtmueller said that although Hutchins created the virus, he spared him jail time. Stadtmueller's ruling noted that Hutchins assisted in stopping the malware and sentenced him to time served and a year of supervised release. (Hornall, Thomas, 2019).

## Malware Types and Attacks

There are millions of malware varieties that threaten computers worldwide. While they exist, they usually come in some recognizable forms. The following are a few typical ways that this virus is delivered and implemented to steal information and damage devices.

There may also be different solutions, depending on the malware you're trying to remedy or defend against, that may be necessary to examine.

*Worms*—This malware predates viruses. Since mainframes were the only computers in existence at the time, worms infected systems. Worms have the ability to copy itself and may spread by capitalizing on flaws through social engineering or in applications. (Walker, Aaron, 2019)

When the system becomes infected, the worm may be able to restrict communication or transfer more malicious software. The functionality of network servers, web servers or single endpoints is affected by worms who are capable of ingesting quite a bit of system memory and render them inhibited.

*Viruses*—The oldest kinds of malware are computer viruses, yet remain important threats in the present day. These computer viruses are distinctive in that they have the ability to replicate without an individual threat actor's control. Entire networks or single computers can be infected by viruses without being properly remedied or quarantined.

*Trojans*—This malicious software is disguised as a computer program that's harmless. However, it has the ability to implement any variety of attacks by providing threat actors that disrupts functionality, steal information, or destroy data.

The name of this software comes from the ancient fable Greek Trojan Horse used to deceive the guards of Troy and had Greek warriors sneak into the city.

*Spyware*—A term coined in the mid-1990s, Spyware defines malware used to get access to the data, files, and behavior of a user's systems and monitor their data. This malware is frequently used to debilitate firewall or anti-malware software increasing an endpoint's vulnerability to attack while ingesting CPU activity to enable the vulnerability.

Spyware monitors the actions of a user by viewing web browsers, collecting data and taking note of local activity. The attacker could either use the data for themselves or sell it for a profit.

Spyware may arrive in the form of keyloggers who track a person's keystrokes. They steal the user's passwords and credentials for data theft or malicious action in the future.

*Macro Virus*—The same macro language is used to write this computer virus, as is used for Microsoft Excel or Microsoft Word. This virus infects a software application, causing a series of actions to immediately begin when the application is opened.

A macro virus works by inserting malicious code in the macros most commonly associated with spreadsheets, documents, and other data files. Opening the document causes malicious programs to run.

Usually, this malware is sent through phishing emails that have attachments that are malicious. When users share documents that are infected, the macro virus spreads. (Rosencrance, 2019)

*File Infecting Virus (also known as File Injector)*— This is a type of malware that infects files that are executable. The intent of this virus is to make the files unusable or create permanent damage.

This virus is the most common and inserts infected code into an executable file or overwrites code. It can spread across a system and over a network to attack and infect other systems. The operating systems this virus can infect include Windows, Macintosh, and Unix. (Techopedia Staff, 2019)

*Polymorphic Virus*—This is a complex file infector that can make modified, different versions of itself so it can avoid detection while retaining the same primary routine after each infection.

Their physical file makeup is varied during every infection and encrypts their codes using different encryption each time. Polymorphic viruses are commonly spread via spam, the use of other malware or infected sites. (Trend Micro Staff, 2019)

It's a shape-changing virus that endlessly replicates itself, sabotaging your system and outwitting your computer. This threat morphs to avoid detection and adapts to defenses you put up against it. (Kaspersky Staff, 2019)

*Stealth Viruses*—This virus attacks the operating system and dodges anti-malware or anti-virus scans. This virus hides in files and is proficient in dodging any detection.

Stealth viruses hide in altered data and other adverse control activities in system memory. It self-copies to computer areas undetected and tricks anti-virus software to avoid being detected.

They also self-modify code by changing the code and virus signature of each file it infects. It also encrypts data and uses a different encryption key for each file infected. (Techopedia Staff, 2019)

*Logic Bomb*—Normally used for malicious purposes, logic bombs can also be used as a timer. Software that is at the end of its free trial date is blocked so a consumer can no longer use the software unless they purchase it at the end of the free trial. If they don't, a trial bomb deactivates the program.

Logic bombs can be excessively damaging should they start cyber wars, a concern of our government and its counterterrorism experts. Due to this concern, the Pentagon developed the U.S. Cyber Command in 2009. This Command was created to be more vigilant about cyber-attacks that could possibly detonate logic bombs and shut down transit and banking systems. (Techopedia Staff, 2019)

*Ransomware*—This form of malware is becoming a very popular way to commandeer a network or computer, requiring payment to restore access to information and endpoints.

Encrypting information and threatening to delete information if the user doesn't pay a ransom is how ransomware holds systems hostage.

A computer becomes infected by ransomware through a Trojan Horse and spreads throughout a network before hijacking control of the endpoints. The ransom usually requires payment in cryptocurrency which makes tracking difficult and offers anonymity to the attacker.

*Adware*—This malware is one of the less damaging malware today. The use of adware is to generate revenue and present users with unwanted ads through a pay-per-click function or display advertising.

Adware is not a predator but more of a pest. End users download the malware tools who then have numerous ads in their web browsers. (Walker, Aaron, 2019)

## How to Protect Yourself from Malware

We now know that malware is malicious, destructive of systems, networks, and data and sneaky. Unfortunately, new versions of malware are always being circulated. They're designed to prevent anti-malware programs from blocking malware from invading and infecting your computer, system, and network.

Installing an anti-malware program on your computer is the first step to protect your computer. Shield yourself with a firewall from the most common malware attacks.

Also, install antivirus software for protection against malware and other threats that make it way past your firewall. (Walker, Aaron, 2019)

# Chapter 13: Best Techniques Against Cyber-Attacks and Damage Control Mechanisms

Cyber-attacks, in the world of data breach, come from external attackers. There are numerous ways that cybersecurity experts work to continue to block attacks. They are also developing software programs that counteract these attacks.

There is research that is ongoing that studies the aftermath of breaches to systems and learn what and how the breach happened so they can develop better protection and damage control mechanisms.

## The Best Practice and Techniques to Prevent Cyber Attacks

*Critical Thinking*—Cybersecurity begins with critical thinking. Cybersecurity specialists have the mindset and skills that give them the capability of anticipating and defending against external and internal threats.

The challenges of working in these quickly changing and complex fields necessitate the ability to reason well in highly precise contexts as well as uncertain and equivocal contexts to have the capability to analyze problems and evaluate alternatives.

Critical Thinking enables Cybersecurity Specialists to:

- Apply algorithmic and quantitative skills
- Make decisions that are high stakes regarding data security
- Manage and assess technology risks
- Plan, evaluate and implement cybersecurity intelligent measures for cybersecurity
- Answer security threats and breaches
- Integrate and identify the latest security intelligence
- Acclimate systems to the continuously changing environment of technology

- Lead the deployment of technology and prevention recover plans

- Clarify threats, options, plans, and progress to co-workers and senior leadership (Insight Assessment, 2019)

*Breach Protocols*—A breach protocol necessitates that the response team (including a third-party technology firm) documents all the steps they implemented to preserve evidence of the breach. They also have to create required detailed reports and disk images for a forensic investigation that is detailed and to avert the same issue from happening again. (Reynold, 2019)

*Training*—SANS cybersecurity training is an indispensable element for individuals and teams to be prepared to protect military, governmental, and commercial institutions from cyber-attacks. (Roussey, 2018)

The skills that cybersecurity experts need for a career in the industry:

- Intrusion detection

- Programming know-how

- Malware analysis and reversing

- Building a well-rounded skillset

- Risk analysis and mitigation

- Cloud security

- Security analysis

- Thinking like a black hat

*Threat Identification*—The process of threat identification examines IT vulnerabilities and decides what their capacity is to harm your system. This is the main element of the risk management program of your organization.

An organization can take preemptive actions identifying threats and are able to obstruct unauthorized users by receiving the information that is needed and prevent system breaches.

*Employee Monitoring*—Data threats from insiders, including intentional destruction or theft of sensitive information, and innocent mistakes that result in the loss of confidential data or control have become, for most businesses, a primary risk factor. Companies need to monitor their employee activities more than ever to protect confidential information.

Tracking the activity of employees requires a balance between a) finding carelessness or wrongdoing by reasonable efforts, that could harm the company and b) the reasonable expectation of privacy, and respecting employees. Moreover, principles have emerged to achieve this balance.

Generally, monitoring employees' activity and communications taking place on a company network can be monitored by the company. For example, software may be employed by employers that look for employees who may be 1) sending confidential company data using their work email and transmitting the information to their personal email accounts 2) using a portable device and downloading large amounts of company data that is sensitive or 3) using phrases that suggests fraud, such as, "let's not discuss this via email, please call me" in their work texts or emails.

It is permissible for an employer to monitor employee phone calls, as long as there is an awareness of this by the employee.

There are several factors making the balance between employee privacy and cybersecurity even more difficult to maintain in years to come.

- There is an increasing number of employees who work from home and use their personal devices for work.

- It has become easier for employers to monitor every keystroke and movement made by the employees thanks to technology.

- Sensitive employee data become public due to the continuation of large hacks and employees' professional and personal lives have become more intertwined, which makes them more interested in having their privacy protected.

- More regulatory pressure to protect their companies from phishing, hacking, and spoofing under more regulatory pressure will increasingly protect employees' personal email accounts and phones from compromise.

There are no quick or easy solutions for a company to find the right balance between employee privacy and company cybersecurity. However, training and having clear policies for employees on using company devices and information and what they should and should not expect to be private can prevent a showdown that could get messy when an employer wishes to access an employee's personal phone and its content and the employee does not want to give permission to do so. (Gesser, 2019)

*Anti-Viruses*—The solution to cybersecurity is anti-virus software that works to prevent, detect, and remove malware from computers and acts as the first line of defense.

Anti-virus software is not a cure-all solution. Unfortunately, there is no infallible software to protect your computer from all threats 100% and that's a reality. However, this is not to disparage anti-virus software, but to have people understand the issues that all software is susceptible to and help them make an informed decision.

## Anti-Virus Software Problems

*Renewal Costs*—Software companies will renew billing annually by auto-billing. In 2009, Symantec and McAfee were subject to a legal suit for charging people's credit cards without gaining permission. They paid $375,000 each for this.

*Anti-Virus Software That's False*—There is a trend of fake software claiming to be anti-virus but is really malware. The Trojan horse is an effective way to trick people in purchasing and then downloading malware that's harmful to their computers.

The removal of these programs is complex and frequently necessitates the assistance of a professional.

## Alternative Protection

There are many alternatives to Anti-virus software, such as hardware and firewalls that protect your system by controlling and monitoring traffic.

Firewalls are good to pair with an Anti-virus program. They can run alongside your current programs to unify your overall security or can replace your anti-virus programs. (Townsend, Caleb, 2019)

*Firewalls*—A firewall monitors and controls incoming and outgoing network traffic predetermined by security rules. Its prime purpose is to establish a barrier between an untrusted external, like the Internet, and a trusted internal network.

Firewalls that are used by companies to protect their devices and data and keep elements that are destructive out of network are Packet filters, Stateful Inspection and Proxy Server Firewalls.

*A Layer 7 Firewall*—This application can be used to accept traffic in a port in general, but obstruct any traffic that contains a vulnerability that's known, such as a malicious telnet command or an SQL injection attack. This would be in place of simply blocking all traffic on a certain port.

*Forensic Analysis*—Forensic analysis is a detailed investigation for the detection and documentation of the reasons, course, culprits, and consequences of a violation of rules of state laws or organization or a security incident.

Specialists of forensic analysis collect various types of information by working with electronic devices as well as in a conventional way with the information written on paper.

*Computer Forensics of Malware*—Malware forensics has become more important with the cybercrime community. Malware attacks create havoc and destruction to retail, financial institutions, and technology.

These cybercrimes are dangerous for governmental and private organizations. Malware is a tool commonly used for installing Trojans, worms, and botnets to the infected device. Responding to malware with speed and accuracy is the only way for organizations to process sensitive information to defend company and client data.

*Computer Forensic Tools*

*Digital Forensics*—Used for gathering and getting evidence from computers.

*Mobile Device Forensics*—Refers to digital forensics involving evidence found on mobile phones, tablets and personal digital assistants (PDAs).

*Software Forensics*—This type of forensics determines if the software has been stolen, analyzes and compares source code, then detects a possible connection.

*Memory Forensics*—Data existing in the hard drive could either have no data left on the hard drive or can be permanently erased when a sophisticated attack happens. This leaves practically no evidence for a forensic investigation.

Searching for possible artifacts in the computer's memory (RAM) is the process of memory forensics. (Comodo, 2018)

*Penetration Testing*—This testing, also call ethical hacking or pen testing is a way of testing a computer system, web application, or network to look for security vulnerabilities that can be exploited by an attacker.

The objective of penetration testing is to identify weaknesses in security. (Rosencrance L. G., 2019)

*Two-Factor Authentication*—called the two-step verification is the combination of something you know—your username and password with something you have, like a physical security key, your phone, or something that's a part of you—like a fingerprint—as a way of confirming that a person is who they say they are.

Two-factor authentication can save your personal data. Security experts state it's one of the best ways for your online accounts to be protected and adds a second step in your normal log-in process.

The two-step factor is important because the days where your single password was a way of protection no longer exists. It also protects you from phishing emails.

The two-step factor is an investment in your security and takes very little time from your day, saving you from a world of problems. (Whittaker, 2018)

## What is Email Protection?

*Email Protection*—Protecting your email is a broad concept that includes many techniques that are all constructed around the protection of digital communications within organizations.

The security measures include login security, spyware detection, and email encryption. Additionally, e-discovery assurance, cloud or on-prem email archival systems, data retention, disaster recovery, and backup.

*Email Security*

One segment of email protection is the methods used to prevent unauthorized compromise or access to email security systems. This includes:

*Login Security*—Numerous methods for protecting email account access from routine password cycling by administrators or best practices training for employees.

*Spam Filtering*—Automated message filtering can avoid fraudulent and malicious emails from arriving employees' inboxes. Spam filtering and automated spear-phishing technology that prevents spam from happening can help identify and quarantine suspicious content to give administrators the ability to determine the risk factor.

*User Security*—The tools to filter email can't catch email attacks that pass by the filters to reach users via their personal email, SMS or voicemail. Educate employees on security awareness.

*Email Encryption*—This is critical for protecting the contents of an email from access from unauthorized cybercriminals as it is accessed for both reading and in archives.

*Employee Education*—Organizations must be sure that employees are trained in best practices for the protection of sensitive data along with implementing the right technologies.

*Virtual Private Network (VPN)*—This is a service that encrypts the traffic on your Internet, protecting your online identity.

Your Internet connection is redirected by a VPN through a remote server run by a VPN provider. The VPN server is your secure launchpad to access the Internet and various websites.

*What Does VPN Do?*

Normally, when accessing a website on the Internet, you begin by connecting to your Internet service provider (ISP). You are then redirected to any websites or other online resources you want to visit.

All your Internet traffic passes through your ISP's servers, allowing anyone to see and log everything you're doing online. Your Internet traffic is redirected through a specially configured remote server. All the data you send or receive is encrypted and the VPN hides your IP address. The data appears to be gibberish to anyone who intercepts it because it's encrypted; it is impossible to read. (Nord VPN, 2019)

*DDoS Protection*—DDoS attacks are high profile and have the potential of consequences that are devastating. Security vendors have begun offering DDoS protection solutions.

DDoS protection uses advanced software and algorithms to screen incoming traffic to the website. Traffic is denied access if it isn't legitimate while legitimate traffic can continue to filter through to the site.

DDoS protection guards against attacks up to a particular size.

*Strong Sign-Off Policy*—In order to be safe and secure from online threats, developing and implementing a strong sign-off policy. Signing off should ensure that laptops and mobile devices should be returned by employees before they leave for the evening. Additionally, the email address being used must be encrypted so data remains confidential and doesn't leak. (Tyler, Alex, 2018)

For a personal computer or mobile device, signing off and shutting down the computer and mobile phone is the safest way to maintain the integrity of your personal and sensitive information.

Leaving it on, especially for long periods of time unattended, can be an open invitation to hackers.

*Protection of Important Data*—To ensure the safety of all information you store is the reason to keep your data protected. Important pieces of information that are normally stored by businesses like customer details, employee records, transactions, or data collection all need to be protected.

Protecting data is to stop data from misuse by attackers for fraud such as phishing scams. Regardless of the data that's being stored either on-site or through a company's servers, keeping data safe should be the number one priority for any company.

Data that needs to be protected:

- Names
- Addresses
- Social Security numbers
- Emails
- Telephone numbers
- Bank and credit card details
- Health information

*Regular System Audits*—A regular IT audit examines and evaluates the infrastructure, organization's information technology, policies, and operations. Due to operations at most modern companies being computerized, IT audits are used to make sure all controls and processes are working properly.

The objectives to do a system audit are:

- Assess the systems and processes that secure company data.

- Weigh the risks to a company's information assets and, to minimize those risks, help identify methods and techniques for protection.

- Make sure that management processes information and is in compliance with IT-specific laws, standards and policies.

- Check for any inefficiencies in IT systems and associated management.

*Cybersecurity Insurance Policy*—Cybersecurity insurance is a product being offered to businesses and individuals to protect them from the effects and results of an online attack. The product is a recognition of the dangers of storing information online.

This insurance is also sold as third-party insurance that covers businesses and individuals that are found to be the responsible party for the breach.

Cybersecurity insurance is a significant risk management tool for tech companies, IT companies, and any other company that stores personal information, particularly information that is sensitive in nature.

This insurance helps to mitigate losses from a data breach, network damage, or other cyber interruption.

*Cyber Risk Assessments*—Cyber risk assessment is a critical part of any company or organization's management of risk strategy. Today, almost every organization depends on information systems and information technology to do business. There are inherent risks in that and, up until the digital age, companies never really had to contend with these types of risks.

The main purpose of a cyber risk assessment is to help support proper risk responses and inform decision-makers of the company. Since most of the CEOs, COIs and the like don't have time to dig into the day-to-day minutiae of cyber operations, a cyber risk assessment will serve as an executive summary to aid those parties to make decisions about security that are informed ones.

To do this, the best way is to identify:

- Pertinent threats to an organization

- External and internal vulnerabilities

- Likelihood of exploitation

- Impact if those vulnerabilities are exploited

*Sandboxing*—Sandboxing is a security mechanism in computer security for separating running programs, usually to diminish software vulnerabilities or system failures from spreading.

It is an isolated environment on a network that copies end-user operating environments. Detecting advanced malware when using a sandbox offers another layer of protection from new threats to security. Malware zero days (previously unseen) and stealthy attacks specifically. (Forcepoint staff, 2019)

## Steps to Take if You've Been Hacked

*Find and Fix the Root Cause*

Root Cause Analysis (RCA) is a technique of problem-solving used to identify the root cause of problems or faults.

There are four steps to RCA:

- Describe and identify the problem clearly. Track the source of the problem.

- Create a timeline from when the situation was normal up to when the problem happened.

- Differentiate between the root cause and other factors.

- Create a casual graph between the root cause and the problem.

RCA usually serves as input to a process where corrective actions are taken to avoid the problem from happening again.

*Conduct a CS-Audit and Maintain a Data Inventory:*

After the issue has been contained, take inventory of all data and perform a cybersecurity audit.

*Review all data throughout the company*—Keep track of all files as to where they are and where they've been. Investigate how services have been used and where sensitive information has traveled.

*See if any files are missing*—Usually, hackers and cybercriminals make copies of files but double-check to see if any files are missing.

*Have any files been released to the public*—Is there is a trail that can show whether any files were leaked and where they went?

These steps may vary and possibly extra steps will be needed, but you need to investigate the problem.

*Damage Control*—Depending on the type of cybersecurity incident that happened and the type of business you in, when a data breach happens, there are different problems that can come up and the need is to get ahead of them.

*Get ahead of the problem before it reaches the public*—If a company has investors or is in involved with the public, do not sweep a data breach under the rug. It will most likely be discovered and hiding it will cost the company more in the long run.

Be honest, explain the problem that's been discovered, that it's being managed, and it will never happen again.

*Change passwords and the methods of verification*—Change both immediately as both are a way of reassuring employees and strengthen security.

*Be proactive*—Protect those affected by identity theft or a breach as a way of mending and protecting the relationships. Providing credit monitoring services is usually a good start to get on the road of mending the relationship.

*Set IT professional time aside*—Answer questions from clients/customers and employees.

*Document everything*—It's possible that legal issues or battles could come about due to the data breach. You will want to be able to make a strong argument in the company's favor.

*Get back to the routine of the company*—Aside from the emphasis of training, you will want to provide great service to maintain your business reputation and credibility.

*Retrain and Refocus*—When things are settled and the business has plans to deal with the problem and avoid it happening in the foreseeable future, it is a good time to review the cybersecurity protocols in general and to offer efficient for employees within the organization.

The moral of the employees will improve and they will feel confident that the issue will not occur again. They will be more receptive to training and feedback on cybersecurity topics.

The training may be refined or refocused. The nature of the breach is what the training will be dependent on. Operations of your business should depend on its cybersecurity or IT professionals. (Phillips, 2017)

# Chapter 14: The Top 10 Largest Cyber Attacks

Although breaches and the seizure of data happens almost daily there is a big difference between small, individual ones and huge company data breaches that span across not just states, but countries worldwide.

This is a compilation of the 10 largest cyber breaches. This list is based on how much damage or risk the breach affected these companies, users, account holders, and insurers.

### 2013-2014 Yahoo

*Affected—3 billion user accounts*

While in the process of negotiating their sale to Verizon in September 2016, Yahoo made it known that it had the largest breach in history in 2014. (Armerding, Taylor, 2018)

The breach amounting to 500 million users included names, email addresses, telephone numbers and dates of birth. A tremendous majority of the passwords involved were hashed by the attack using the powerful bcrypt algorithm.

Just two months later in December 2016, Yahoo revealed that there had been a previous breach in 2013. It was hacked by a different group. 1 billion accounts were compromised. There were the users' security questions compromised along with names, dates of birth, email addresses, and passwords that were not as protected.

By October 2017, Yahoo stated, after revising their estimate, that 3 billion user accounts had been compromised.

Unfortunately, per a new investigation conducted internally, Yahoo knew of the massive data breach but did not respond appropriately. Senior executives and Yahoo's security team were aware of the hack of certain accounts in 2014. Even after adding new security features and notifying 26 users that were targeted in the hack so of these executives did not understand or bother to investigate the incident any further.

Verizon did eventually purchase Yahoo for $4.48 billion, but the breaches reduced the sale price by $350 million. In their sale agreement, both Verizon and Yahoo will share legal and regulatory liabilities from breaches.

## 2014-2018 Marriott International

*Affected–500 million customers*

Marriott International announced in November 2018 that there had been data stolen by cyber thieves of approximately 500 million customers.

The systems that supported the Starwood hotel brands were where the breach actually occurred beginning in 2014. Marriott acquired Starwood in

2016 during which the attackers remained in the system. The breach was not discovered until September 2018.

Names and contact information was not the only data compromised for some of the victims. Seized passport numbers, personal information, and the Preferred Guest of Starwood accounts were also compromised.

100 million customers' personal information was stolen, although Marriott cannot ascertain if there was an ability to decipher credit card information.

A group that wanted to collect personal information on U.S. individuals was attributed to the crime. This was the largest breach of personal information known.

## October 2016 Adult Friend Finder

*Affected–412.2 million accounts plus*

The FriendFinder Network, a series of adult content and casual hookup websites including Penthouse.com, Adult Friend Finder, iCams.com, Cams.com, and Stripshow.com suffered a data breach sometime in October 2016.

Six databases with 20 years of data were attacked. Hackers seized data information of the websites' users. The majority of the data were protected by SHA-1, a weak algorithm, meaning that 99% of the passwords had been opened when the analysis of LeakedSource.com was published in November 2014.

Diana Ballou, Vice President of AFF issued a statement saying the company identified and fixed the vulnerability giving the ability to access source code.

**May 2014 eBay**

*Affected–145 million users compromised*

A cyber-attack in May 2014 was reported by the online auction website stating that the attack compromised all the personal information including encrypted passwords of its 145 million users at that time.

Credentials of three corporate employees were used by the attackers hacking into the company network allowing them complete access inside eBay's system for over 7.5 months. The hackers were able to get to the eBay database.

Customers were advised to make changes to their passwords and stated that their financial information, which was stored separately, was not compromised.

The poor communication and execution in alerting its users—the renewal process of the password renewal had eBay receive criticism from the public. The poor response resulted in user activity declining. However, eBay's bottom line increased by 13 percent, with no loss, and in line with the expectations of analysts.

## July 29, 2017, Equifax

*Affected–143 million consumers*

One of the largest credit bureaus in the United States, Equifax reported that on September 7, 2017, a breach impacted approximately 147.9 million consumers to a data breach caused by vulnerability on one of their websites.

The discovery of the breach occurred on July 29th, but according to the company, the breach likely began sometime in mid-May 2017.

After further investigation, Equifax increased its number of estimated consumers affected by the breach to 145.5 million. There was an additional revised total of consumers affected by the breach on March 1, 2018. An additional 2.4 million was added to the total consumers affected to make it a grand total of 147.9 million consumers affected.

Equifax launched a website for those consumers possibly impacted by the breach and has offered credit monitoring to all consumers in the U.S. Additionally, Equifax hired a forensics firm to assist in investigating and provide direction to avoid this type of breach from occurring again.

## March 2008 Heartland Payment Systems

*Affected–134 million credit cards*

Heartland Payment Systems had 134 million compromised credit cards via SQLi installed spyware their data systems.

Heartland was processing transactions of 100 million payment cards monthly mostly small and mid-sized retailers, at the time of the breach, totaling 175,000 merchants.

The breach was not detected until MasterCard and Visa notified Heartland in January 2009 of transactions from accounts appeared to be suspicious transactions.

Heartland was banned and deemed out of compliance until May 2009 and was blocked from processing major credit cards. Additionally, an estimated $145 million was paid for fraudulent payments by the company as compensation.

Although security analysts had warned retailers about their vulnerability, many Web-facing applications and the continuing vulnerability made SQLi the usual attacker against websites at that time. (Armerding, Taylor, 2018)

Albert Gonzalez, the star hacker mastermind of the Heartland breach was arrested and convicted with 11 others for stealing credit card information.

Gonzalez was working for the U.S. Secret Service as a paid informant garnering a salary of $75,000 at the time of the crimes.

The government claimed that banks, companies, and insurers lost $200 million because of this beach. (Armerding, Taylor, 2018)

## December 2013 Target

*Affected–110 million consumers' credit and debit card information and/or contact information*

This breach occurred in 2013, just before Thanksgiving. However, it was not detected until several weeks later. Initially, the retailer reported access was gained via a vendor to the card readers at the point-of-sale. Hackers gathered approximately 40 million credit and debit card numbers.

However, in January 2014, the estimated number of consumers affected increased to 70 million of its customers have had their identifiable information taken. The final estimate of the breach affected 110 million customers.

The company reported the cost of the breach was $162 million.

## December 2006 TJX Companies, Inc.

*Affected–94 million credit cards exposed*

A large retailer, TJX Companies has 2,000 retail stores such as Marshalls, T.J. Maxx, Bob's Stores, HomeGoods, and A.J. Wright.

There are questions and conflicting reports on how this breach actually occurred.

One report supposes that hackers attacked the data encryption system that was weak and stole credit card data during a wireless transfer in Miami, FL. between two of Marshall's stores.

Another report is an in-store kiosk, which allows people to electronically apply for a job, was hacked giving the hackers the ability to break into the TJX network.

**Late 2016 Uber**

*Impact—57 million Uber customers personal information*

The extent of the breach was not the worst of the hack, but it is how Uber handled the breach once it was detected. It is a study on how companies should not handle a breach.

Two hackers in late 2016 had accessed the names, personal information and phone numbers of 57 million customers who were Uber app users.

Along with customer information, the hackers obtained 600,000 Uber drivers' license numbers but did not compromise their credit card or Social Security information.

Uber's GitHub account was accessed by hackers and information compromised.

Uber did not make the breach public for a year. Even worse, the hackers were paid $100,000 by Uber to destroy the data saying it was a "bug bounty" fee.

The breach, and the way it was handled cost Uber not only money but their reputation as well. The company had been in negotiations to sell a share of the company to Softbank.

Uber's value was $68 billion, but the company's valuation had dropped to

$48 billion. The breach was not the total reason the valuation was reduced, but it was a significant factor.

## July 2014 JP Morgan Chase

*Affected–83 million small businesses and households*

JP Morgan Chase is the largest bank in the U.S. with $2.5 trillion in assets and, during the summer of 2014, was the victim of a hack that compromised the data of 7 million small businesses, with the possibility of countless of customers affected, and more than half of the U.S. households–76 million.

Names, addresses, email addresses, telephone numbers, and internal information about users was the data compromised, according to a filing with the SEC (Securities and Exchange Commission).

There was no indication of money stolen and no indication of account information affected such as bank account numbers, passwords, user IDs, Social Security numbers, and other personal information was compromised.

The hackers still had the ability to attain "root" privileges having the ability to take actions including closing accounts and transferring funds on more than 90 of the bank's servers.

These are just 10 of the largest data breaches to date. What stands out about some of these breaches is the length of time it took for them to be detected by the companies that were attacked.

This demonstrates just how pervasive and sophisticated the viruses and malware are when they are able to pinpoint weakness and make their way into computers, systems, and networks of major corporations.

IT Security companies and the creators of security software must stay in step with the malware software that is consistently updated to perpetrate data breaches such as these.

# Chapter 15: The General Data Protection Regulation (GDPR)

The GDPR became effective on May 25, 2018, replacing the Data Protection Directive.

GDPR grew and, more specifically, defined requirements that, as a new controlling structure, the GDPR was a recognition that the digital economy, powered by personal information, should function with the informed permission of users and rules that are clear for companies who look to do business with the European Union.

This policy, the first of its kind, was developed to help EU citizens better comprehend how their personal information was being used and to standardize the data and privacy protection laws across Europe.

The GDPR encouraged EU citizens that, if they felt their rights were violated, to file a complaint. It also permits a citizen's right to be forgotten. This structure represents data privacy regulation, the sweeping change in decades.

The GDPR principles are

- Lawfulness
- Fairness and transparency
- Data minimization
- Purpose limitation.

*Effect on Business*—Although there was existing legislation already in place that delivered a reasonably high level of privacy protection, the GDPR extended the range of this criterion to non-EU organizations that process Europeans' personal data.

With the passage of GDPR, two organizations were founded, NYOB (for none of your business) a Non-Governmental Organization (NGO) who filed the first complaints against non-European organizations as soon as the GDPR went into effect.

Another NGO, La Quadrature du Net, also filed some of the initial complaints against Google, Apple, Facebook, Amazon, and Microsoft (GAFAM).

These complaints, in total of 12,000 French citizens, were consequently made available as templates to reuse by others in the EU.

The GDPR exposed the obtaining of consent and how low the bar was for transparency. As a result of the joint complaints from NYOB and La Quadrature du Net, Google was fined €50 million ($55.3 million) by CNIL, a French data protection authority for forcing user consent providing only one choice—full consent to non-specific uses of users' data, which was poorly explained, or do not proceed at all.

*Effects on Consumers*—The GDPR individual rights are:

- to be informed...

- of access,

- of erasure,

- of rectification,

- to data portability,

- to restrict processing,

- to object,

- rights related to automated profiling, and

- decision making

The GDPR is a success as an example of a breach notification policy. The policy states that when a breach occurs, within 72 hours the 'supervisory authority' must be notified with the fundamental goal that users who were affected be notified so they can take steps to protect their private and sensitive information, and themselves. (Herrle, 2019)

The GDPR set a strong example and let loose a repressed demand for the U.S. rules and regulations to protect the data of consumers. (Sword & Shield Enterprise Security, 2019)

There are provisions that focus on an individuals' right to maintain their data from being subjected to automated decision making, such as profiling.

The provision against profiling by the GDPR in decision making that is automated states that, if the user consents, profiling may be allowed.

Many Europeans' awareness of data privacy and protection increased, and at least one of their new rights have been heard of and recognized by 73% of the people. However, only three in ten Europeans are cognizant of all of their rights.

There has been an upswing of people exercising their rights. 144,000 individual complaints (regarding access requests, employee privacy and deletion requests, and unwanted marketing and advertising have been filed.

The GDPR also brought a significant awareness of the many shortcomings or possible flaws regarding data protection in many cities' plans and has made the entire idea of privacy as a human right, something that had not been possessed before. (Herrle, 2019)

*Research and development*—The GDPR's impact on research is that it was not designed to hinder research and allows research particular privileges. There is a recognition that research can be a long-term enterprise and that data can be useful for research.

Storage limitations, as long as other data protection and particular protections are met, can exempt research.

The GDPR law demands that the processing of data is fair, lawful, and transparent. The most important changes surround transparency requirements and meeting the necessary protections.

Personal data is related to people who are living from which, through the data itself, direct identifiability, or from the combination of data with other available data, indirect identifiability. The International Commissioner's Office (ICO) offers guidance on this.

Organizations that control data processing or process personal data are accountable for complying with legislation through their research management functions and Data Protection officers. (Ukri.org, 2018)

*Government*—At this writing, the GDPR has been in effect for one year. Since that time, lawmakers, CEOs, and lobbyists in the U.S. are looking to throw out what they feel is the worst of this privacy law and cherry-pick what they feel are the best parts of the EU law.

Since then, Facebook, Apple, and Google have asked for comprehensive privacy legislation, similar to GDPR on a federal level.

Some states have gone ahead and instituted their own form of the EU law because privacy legislation is a rare bipartisan topic in Congress.

The U.S. has praise for GDPR, but they also point to its flaws.

Privacy supporters and regulators signaled the legislation victorious for consumers who, in the aftermath of scandals like Cambridge Analytica, wanted more control over their personal data.

The EU rules give traction to the enforcement of privacy regulations. Fines of up to 20 million euros or 4% of annual revenues, whichever is the greater, are the fines companies face if they breach GDPR regulations.

Currently, there have not been any billion-dollar fines levied, while users and companies are frustrated by the complexity of the law.

U.S. lawmakers, CEOs, and lobbyists want to acclimatize many of the securities under GDPR but find streamlining those requirements to comply under GDPR are difficult.

Website banners to 'opt-in' can hurt users' online involvement, while there are significant penalties for smaller businesses.

Companies are for the individual rights under the GDPR such as correction, transparency, access to data, and deletion.

Currently, there is a need for an overall national standard rather than a patchwork of laws that expect users to understand what rights they have and that they are consistent rights.

Officials in Europe are hard at work decoding the GDPR and its complexity, particularly for smaller companies. One critique of the law is that smaller businesses have been left to struggle with understanding compliance while large tech companies who have copious legal resources can more easily comply or even pay fines.

Any company that has customers in the EU, even if the business' headquarters are outside the alliance, are subject to GPDR and all its regulations.

Although it would be an easy way to assure privacy rights with a uniform standard, it doesn't seem an international agreement is likely at this time.

The goal to arrive at is having a global consensus on privacy, but it is a few years away. That is, however, where everyone would like it to be. (Schulze, Elizabeth, 2019)

# Chapter 16: The Future Of Cybersecurity

## What is the future of Cybersecurity?

What is the future of cybersecurity? With the sophistication and refinement of viruses and malware software, how will cybersecurity stack up to the demand to be vigilant against the potential for attacks?

There are several aspects to how cybersecurity will make its way into the future. The utmost priority is to provide the highest form of security to ward of cyber-attacks, driving businesses to focus on cybersecurity and the future.

The future of cybersecurity is having the ability to take advantage of machine learning and artificial intelligence.

Developing more sophisticated new tools and methods to have the ability to gain access to private information will be continued by hackers. As technology evolves, this will provide hackers an enormous attack surface and give them the ability to exploit more vulnerabilities.

In the past, company security teams could concentrate on on-premise systems. However, they now need to focus on the cloud with AWS, Azure, and all the tools that have sensitive information or could offer a path to compromise other information.

## Artificial Intelligence (AI)–What It Is

Artificial Intelligence–AI is the area of computer science that underscores the creation of intelligent machines. These machines react and work like humans.

They are able to perform tasks that usually need human intelligence. The activities some computers with AI are designed to have included:

- Learning

- Speech recognition

- Visual perception

- Planning

- Translation between languages

- Decision-making

- Problem-solving

## AI and Cybersecurity

61% of companies are unable to detect breach attempts today without using AI technologies.

48% have plans to increase their budget for the Fiscal Year (FY) 2020 for AI in cybersecurity by an average of 29%.

Cisco has reported breach attempts and in 2018 their cybersecurity blocked seven trillion threats protecting their customers.

A survey of 850 senior executives from around the world was conducted by Capgemini's Research Institute, a think tank doing research on cybersecurity. The executives represented seven industries including consumer products, banking, insurance, retail, utilities, automotive, and telecom.

Of the executives surveyed, 20% were Chief Information Officers (CIO) and
10% were Chief Information Security Officers (CISO). Companies with headquarters in Europe, the U.S., Netherlands, India, and Sweden were all included in the report Capgemini produced from their survey on cybersecurity.

It was found that as digital businesses continue to expand, the risk of cyber-attacks would increase enormously.

Of all the enterprises surveyed, 21% stated their company had experienced a cybersecurity breach that led to unauthorized access in 2018. Add in the losses due to breach of security, and the price they're paying is a hefty one.

Cybersecurity breaches have cost 20% of companies who have experienced a breach have reported losses of more than $50 million. Centrify, a cybersecurity company, stated that it found 74% of all breaches have involved access to a privileged access account.

A popular method that hackers use to begin a breach, uses privileged access credentials, which pulls out valuable data from company systems and sells it on the Dark Web.

Almost 70% of companies have determined that artificial intelligence will be needed to respond to cyber-attacks. 80% of telecom companies say they are depending on AI to aid in identifying threats and counter-attacks.

Company executives are focusing their time and budgets on having cyber threats detected using AI above predicting and responding, say 64% of companies. Using AI reduces the cost to companies to detect and respond.

It also diminishes the total time taken to actually detect breaches and threats by 12%, while the number of time attackers, known as dwell time, that remain undetected has dropped by 11% using AI. (Columbus, 2019)

The most important uses for AI are fraud detections, intrusion detection, malware detection, user/machine behavioral analysis, and scoring risk in a network.

*Big Data*

Big data is a term used in describing a very large data set. It is mined and evaluated to check for patterns and trends of behavior. It is described as being dense in velocity, variety, and volume. (the University of San Diego, n.d.)

Big data has introduced new potentials by way of security solutions and analytics to help protect data and prevent any future cyber-attacks. However, it has also given cybercriminals the ability to access vast amounts of personal and sensitive information through the use of advanced technology.

Three major challenges that many businesses are having with big data:

- Sensitive and personal information is protected
- Data ownership and rights
- Unable to have data scientists available to analyze the data

The security and technologies used to mine data and prevent cyber-attacks are traditionally more reactive than proactive. This has created numerous false positives that have distracted from actual threats and created inefficiencies.

Big data analytics, as a comparison, gives professionals of cybersecurity the capability to analyze data from numerous different and data types and sources and respond in real-time.

Big data has the capability to connect the dots between data and making comparisons and connections that otherwise may have been missed while gathering information from an enormous universe.

With big data, cybercrime professionals increase their efficiency and cast a net that is far-reaching and more reliable when it comes to preventing cyber-attacks. (the University of San Diego, n.d.)

*Quantum Technology*

What does quantum technology mean for the future of cybersecurity? It means that one 'unit' will be able to hold a larger quantity of information than the present-day classical computing. A unit has the potential to be more energy-efficient and faster than the computers that have been used.

Quantum computers will permit quick integration and analysis of extremely large data sets which will transform and improve machine learning and the capabilities of artificial intelligence.

The processing speed of Quantum computing is because qubits are more efficient in carrying data and is much faster than classical computers. Large amounts of data can be handled, and big problems can be resolved.

Quantum devices have approximately 20 qubits, is the largest commercial quantum device for now, although Google introduced the largest quantum computer to date with 72 qubit processor in March 2018. Prior to Google's unveiling, IBM had the largest 50 qubit processor. The race to build a quantum computer that will be the world's first useful one is very near the end. (Greene, 2018)

**The Future of Ransomware**

Ransomware, as was pointed out in Chapter 12, was at its peak with the WannaCry cyber-attack of 2017 but has remained quiet and people were not really taking ransomware precautions because it was not active.

However, people are still being targeted for attacks by injection, phishing attacks, malware, and virus, clearly an indication that cybercriminals and cyberbullies, for their benefit, are continuing using ransomware attacks that are hostile.

Although there are those who think that the era of ransomware attacks has fallen to the wayside, think again—it appears that health associations are now being targeted.

Due to the forceful activities of cybercriminals, the health industry is facing a crisis in gathering data in one place. While hackers are aiming to get their hands-on patent data, the health industry is working to prevent malicious attacks from cybercriminals from gaining entry into the crucial data and system.

In 2017, the WannaCry attack was global, affecting healthcare organizations including the National Health Service of the United Kingdom for over a week, resulting in thousands of appointments being canceled, operations delayed, emergency patients impacted and patient records totally disappearing.

Companies and healthcare organizations are well aware of how destructive ransomware is and work every day to prevent the type of global attack that was perpetrated on their systems and networks. (Tweaklibrary Team, 2019)

*Botnet Attacks*

Botnet computers that form a group are connected in coordination for malicious attacks. The individual computers, called bots, fall under the control of cybercriminals.

Gaining control of these individual computers usually begins with a virus, and then they are connected into a giant army of bots, creating a network of computers tied together by the virus.

Botnets launch extensive attacks like (DDoS), a coordinated distribution of an attack, or spam campaigns that are done on a large scale.

It is possible that the owners of the computers being used in this illegal activity are not aware that their computers are being used and are known as Zombie computers or bots. Mirai, a botnet, has demonstrated the future of botnets is IoT. The Mirai botnet was the idea of two teenagers who were playing a game called Minecraft. They were looking to get a competitive edge in the game.

Their idea grew into an army of connected Internet of Things (IoT) that includes routers and digital cameras.

In 2016 the Internet domain company, Dyn, had a massive DDoS attack resulting in the failure of Netflix, Twitter, CNN and many other large corporations and Europe.

New variants have popped regularly up since the Dyn attack. Mirai has continued with reports surfacing about new Mirai malware samples. Researchers have found an increase in the number of devices that can be added to the Mirai botnet.

The number of IoT devices have grown. IP cameras, printers, wearables, and building controls and a variety of other smart devices are used at both home and at work. They all represent a possibility for botnet control and consequently, a source for huge DDoS attacks and other criminal activity with an

Internet connection built into each device. (Mayfield, 2019)

## Data Weaponization

This is an important threat to everyone's security and privacy. Organizations have gathered vast amounts of personal data of users as a part of their daily operations. This data can be valuable in providing the services by improving them and what they offer. That is if it is used for its intended purpose.

There have been, however, recent events that have demonstrated that collected data has been gathered by organizations for purposes that were not expected by the customers, nor were they authorized.

Free social media platforms immediately come to mind. They are supposed to fund themselves by running advertising, but they frequently sell the user data as a supplement to the platform's income.

Facebook and Cambridge Analytica are prime examples.

Simply put, don't put any of your data that is personal and sensitive where it has the potential of being collected. This includes any of your devices that connect to the Internet. This is a way of protecting yourself from data weaponization.

This is almost impossible however in today's world. Your doctor, bank, credit card company, and more all possess your sensitive and personal information.

The best solution is minimizing the amount of data placed on platforms that are untrusted and insecure. (Sword & Shield Enterprise Security, 2019)

## Satellite Attacks

Artificial intelligence is being used by the National Security Agency (NSA) to typify small satellites and their strange behaviors to comprehend if they been brought under adversarial control secretly.

The NSA is seeking a way to typify telemetry data so when new satellites are sent out, adjustments can be made.

A variety of analysts at NASA will say that data has been checked two, even three times, and that the satellites' data is under control.

However, there is really no way of knowing because there is an abundance of data that will not let them know if something is going wrong. NASA will state that if there is a sense of something being wrong, they explain the satellite was bumped by orbital debris and that's what knocked it off its course.

Can small sat behaviors be characterized to be good or bad—or no one knows?

Currently, the NSA is looking into how they can send some type of malware to a smallsat to judge threats to small satellites.

The importance of this is the discussion by the military to use space in the next two years. There are two key points in this plan.

The United States is to deploy in low Earth orbit vast constellations of small satellites in the coming years. This will provide new and faster ways to collect intelligence for the military and to communicate.

The United States has become extremely worried about new and growing threats to their assets in space, and the enormous volume of data emitting from small satellites make it hard to decipher if an adversary has compromised the satellites.

The solution is to have a more diversified and elaborate design of satellites, both large and small;

developing a one size does not fit all approach. (Tucker, Patrick, 2019)

## Attacks on Government

During 2018, in the U.S. alone, there were 99 military and government data breaches. In May 2019, Baltimore was attacked–online payment processing was halted, city email service shut down, and transactions of real estate could not be recorded.

The hackers demanded an estimated $100,000 in bitcoins.

Agencies of the government, particularly on the municipal, local, and state levels don't have expansive resources. Underfunded and understaffed have cybersecurity wanting for attention. Because of their vulnerability, they are considered easy targets that can provide a wealth of private and sensitive data the cybercriminals can hold for ransom or sell on the Dark Net.

The question becomes what do governments do in the event of a ransomware attack–pay the ransom or fight for what is rightfully theirs?

Unfortunately, government agencies frequently receive advice that can be conflicting. Officials with law enforcement feel ransoms shouldn't be paid because it can attract other attacks.

There is the possibility that a victim can pay the ransom, but there is no guarantee that agencies will have the ability to retrieve their information.

In the case of NotPetya in June 2017, a ransomware attack that crippled seaports, immobilized corporations, and froze government agencies, the result was $10 billion in total damages and practically wiped out all of the data of several industries and companies.

There are other times that hackers may give back access to functions and data, but entire systems must be rebuilt to make sure that no ransomware remained and any traces of it were gone.

In order to diminish downtime and damage, and avoid having to pay a ransom, agencies should consider what is at stake if a hacker does succeed in seizing data, systems, and networks.

Having an inventory conducted of all assets owned will permit agencies to be aware of what has been affected and have the ability to restore and recover all data.

Proactive management and preventative action, IT professionals and users being trained and technological excellence to fight against cyber-attacks are ways of increasing cybersecurity. Information security staff should take the lead in finding and fixing cybersecurity weaknesses.

Educating staff is a high priority. Awareness training will point out and strengthen any weak links from within.

Finally, the information security staff must be proactive and continuously keep up with the latest in cybersecurity practices and developments.

Needless to say, companies in many of the major industries of finance, telecommunications, retailers, and the like will be continuing to have a watchful eye on all the technology that will aid in thwarting cyber-attacks. (Canellos, 2019)

## What Consequences Does the Average User Face?

Cybersecurity Ventures online https://cybersecurityventures.com/ headlines that cybercrime damages are predicted to reach $6 trillion by 2021. They don't mince words on cybercriminal activity being one of the largest challenges that will be faced by humanity in the coming twenty years.

According to Cybersecurity Ventures, the cost has risen from $3 trillion in 2015 to an expected $6 trillion by 2021. Cybercrime is fast becoming one of the most lucrative ways to make money and outdoing the sale of all illegal drugs combined.

The prediction for a rise in cybercrime has been validated by industry experts, cybercrime fighters worldwide, media outlets, and cybersecurity and technology companies.

The fastest growing crime in the U.S. is cyber-attacks and is on the rise in sophistication and cost. Cybercrime is an epidemic that has hit the U.S. intensely. It is also predicted that the total amount of data stored in the cloud and operated by vendors and social media companies will be a hundred times greater by 2021.

Internet of Things (IoT) world will blow up from 2 billion objects–smart devices communicating wirelessly–in 2006 and are projected to increase to 200 billion by 2020, not to mention that 300 billion passwords will have to be cyber protected globally by 2020.

## Digital Transformation

Organizations have had a digital transformation on the agenda for a number of years and it is predicted that 2018-2020 will be a key time for industry leaders to plan for and execute it.

There is extensive recognition that digital technology's role is shifting.

The shift is from driving marginal efficiency to being a facilitator of disruption and innovation.

In the years coming up, 85% of decision-makers feel they need to get a grip with digital transformation. There is an urgency.

Digital transformation will dominate business strategy and CEOs will look to their Chief Information Officers (CIOs) to be a strategic partner and guide companies through significant changes.

Spending in the tech industry has increased and has exceeded globally $3 trillion for the first time ever, and $1.5 trillion in the U.S.

This is an age dominated by the consumer. Needed is implementing technology that can measure, track, and respond to important shifts in consumer behavior. This could make or break a business.

AI and automation are augmenting the workforce to offer superior levels of efficiency. This shift will give the Chief Marketing Officer the ability to take charge of growth.

There is a need to prepare for big changes. The evolution of digital use and the impact it will have on businesses worldwide will be the concern seeking to cement their place in the future.

AI and ML technology will remain to be a tremendous force in the business world, meaning CEOs, CIOs, and CMOs must all commit to new operating models that will actually be added value to the company.

## Future Political Regulations

Privacy and cybersecurity issues are rapidly moving to the head of Homeland Security, and State importance, and State-Federal policies.

Cybersecurity legislation has been introduced and posted on the National Conference of State Legislatures (NCSL):

*Political Regulations*

In 2019, 43 states and Puerto Rico considered or introduced approximately 300 bills or resolutions that deal with cybersecurity. Additionally, cybersecurity-related legislation was enacted by thirty-one states.

Some of the areas that are key to legislative activity are:

- Government agencies or businesses are required to implement specific types of practices and security policies or training

- Commissions or task forces to be created

- Improve security by restructuring government

- Study the use of blockchain for cybersecurity

- Provide protection of utilities and critical infrastructure

- Provide funding for security measures improvement

- The insurance industry to regulate cybersecurity

- Address connected device security

- Exempt cybersecurity operations information from laws in the public records

- Addressing the threats to cybersecurity to elections

Continually investing in the protection of state networks from cyber-attacks and securing them with strong cyber policies will benefit the states. (NCSL, 2019)

# Conclusion

Thank you for reading **Cybersecurity For Beginners**!

Hopefully, it was informative and able to provide you with all of the tools you need to be more aware of the benefits of cybersecurity and how it is imperative that you safeguard your personal and sensitive information as much as possible.

Although many people have heard of cybersecurity and the various breach of organizations, or have experienced their own breach of a device, there are still those who believe it can only happen to the next guy and are not taking enough precautions to guard against a cyber-attack.

Even if you're a beginner and have never paid attention to what cybersecurity is all about, this book has now given you the information you need to protect yourself and your family from having your devices attacked and the data you and they hold compromised.

The good news is this book has shown that a simple update of software and/or ridding your devices of unnecessary or unwanted plug-ins can be the thing that keeps your devices safe. Adding software specifically designed to ward off viruses and malware is also a plus in protection.

The reality is, if you suffer a personal breach of your personal device, it's not only your information that is compromised but the information of others who communicate with you as well. It's not a pleasant thought, but there are ways to aid in protecting yourself.

**Cybersecurity For Beginners** explained what cybersecurity is, the types of attacks that have been and are still being used by hackers. Getting instructions on how to configure security settings for the three most popular browsers, is a plus and should be applied to all your devices.

All those words we read or hear about such as cryptography or encryption that haven't made much sense now have more clarity and will now make sense to any novice.

Additionally, with the major breaches of the 21st century that have happened, cybersecurity experts are continuing to study and then implement more and stronger protection of major organizations' computers. Even if, in some cases, a cyber-criminal can penetrate an outer layer of an organization's system, there are more ways that have been developed to block malware or other types of attacks from having the ability to get any further.

The next step is to take inventory of your personal computers, laptops, tablets, and cell phones to see how vulnerable they are. Once you recognize the vulnerabilities, you will be able to address them and shore up any possible openings that a hacker can attack.

This book has tried to encompass all the information about cybersecurity and the hazards that can disrupt you personally, as well as doing the same to major organizations worldwide. Cybersecurity is a top-of-mind topic and will continue to be into the next millennium.

Finally, if you found this book useful in any way, a review on Amazon is highly appreciated!

Reviews are crucial for a book to survive on Amazon. Hence, we as authors heavily depend on them.
So, if you found this book useful in any way, I would be delighted to see a review from you with a simple feedback on what you liked and what could be improved.

Thank you so much for reading to the end of this book, and good luck with your endeavors in the world of cybersecurity!

# 9 Stunning And Free Cyber-Attack Maps

*Definition*—A map showing cyber-attacks map is a way to show graphically demonstrate how the Internet functions. Each day millions of new victims are impacted by cyber threats. Some perform retaliations while others justify the attacks and remain passive.

*Maps*

*FireEye Cyber Threat Map*—The map only shows origin, destination and the total number of attacks. Included are statistics covering the previous 30 days like topmost attacked industries and attacker countries.
https://www.fireeye.com/cyber-map/threat-map.html

*Kaspersky Cyber Malware and DDoS Real-Time Map*—This threat map is one of the most complete maps of its kind. It detects your current location once you load the map and indicates statistics for your country. It also includes local infections for the last week.

https://cybermap.kaspersky.com/widget/

*Trend Micro*—Trend Micro cyber-attack map is a smaller map tracking C&C (Command and Control) servers used by botnets (and global targets). Historical data tracks back 14 days. (Ragan, Steve, 2017)

https://botnet-cd.trendmicro.com/

*Akamai Real-Time Web Attack Monitor*—The map focuses on the highest attack locations for the past 24 hours. It allows a choice between different regions of the world; the Americas, Europe, the Middle East, Asia Pacific, Africa, and Japan. https://www.akamai.com/fr/fr/resources/visualiz ing-akamai/real-time-web-monitor.jsp

*Digital Attack Map*–When you watch daily DDoS attacks worldwide, you can filter the map with multiple options:

By attack size:

- Large

- Combined

- Unusual

By attack type:

- TCP Connection (filling connections)

- Fragmentation (pieces of packets)

- Volumetric (eating bandwidth)

- Source & destination port number

- Application

- Duration

DDoS is perilous to your online business. It can destroy your online presence and hurt financially, as well as the business' reputation.

If you are a web administrator or business owner, then you need to protect your online assets from DDoS by using services like Cloudflare, SUCURI. https://www.digitalattackmap.com/#anim=1&color=0&country=ALL&list=0&time=18181&view=map

*Threatbutt*—Threat Butt provides a digital attack map that's the best, because its design is retro, and includes the Atari sound.

The map is black and green in the design. Lines, where attacks are detected in different countries, extend in red lines. Description and attack information, including countries of origin, IP address, and captions are noted below the map. https://threatbutt.com/map/

*Check Point Software*—The ThreatCloud cyber-attack map exhibits historical data. It is reset each day at 12:00 am PST. Along with playback, top targets and attackers can be viewed with weekly and monthly stats.

https://threatmap.checkpoint.com/

(Ragan, Steve, 2017)

*Fortinet*—Incoming and outgoing attack, country-based statistics and general activity can be located by clicking on any country's name. The type of attack is seen in the map by different colors, for example:

http://threatmap.fortiguard.com/

(Security Trails, 2019)

- Execution—remote execution attacks

- Link—attack from a remote location

- DoS—Denial of service attacks

- Memory—memory-related attacks

- Generic attacks

*Deteque9*—A botnet attack map that offering mass amounts of valuable information. Areas with the activity of high botnet and probable botnet command and control servers are identified. The more bots are active at a location, the larger the circle on the map.

When fully zoomed out, the map may appear messy, but it can be zoomed in on any location to look at details on the attacks in the targeted area.

Click on a dot on the map to see the names of the bots, how many there are and the location.

IT specialists can find this map to be a valuable tool for tracking botnet attacks in a specific location. https://www.deteque.com/live-threat-map/

Must know Cybersecurity-facts for 2019:

https://www.varonis.com/blog/cybersecurity-statistics/